Mallorca

by Tony Kelly

Tony Kelly first visited Mallorca on a
walking holiday in 1995 and he has been
returning to the island ever since. In 2000 he
was awarded a diploma by the Mallorca
Tourist Board for his writing 'reflecting the
true spirit and diverse nature of Mallorca'.
An expert on Spain, his other guidebooks
include *AA Essential Menorca*, *Essential
Costa Brava* and *Spiral Gran Canaria*.
He lives near Cambridge with his wife
and young son.

Above: *Cala Sant Vicenç*

D0233788

Written by Tony Kelly

First published 1998. Reprinted November 1998.
Second edition January 2000. Reprinted Feb, Apr, Aug and
Oct 2000, May 2001.
Reprinted April 2002. Information verified and updated.
Reprinted Aug 2002. Reprinted Jun 2003.
This edition 2004. Reprinted May 2004

Published by AA Publishing, a trading name of Automobile
Association Developments Limited, whose registered
office is Millstream, Maidenhead Road, Windsor, Berkshire
SL4 5GD. Registered number 1878835.

Colour separation: BTB Digital Imaging Limited,
Whitchurch, Hampshire

Printed and bound in Italy by Printer Trento S.r.l.

A02230

*Above: Catalina Thomas,
patron saint of Mallorca,
depicted on a tile set on
the side of a house in her
home town of Valldemossa*

Find out more about
AA Publishing and the
wide range of travel
publications and services
the AA provides by
visiting our website at
www.theAA.com

Contents

About this Book

KEY TO SYMBOLS

✚ map reference to the maps found in the What to See section (see below)

✉ address or location

☎ telephone number

🕐 opening times

🍴 restaurant or café on premises or near by

🚇 nearest underground train station

🚌 nearest bus/tram route

🚆 nearest overground train station

🚢 ferry crossings and excursions by boat

✈ travel by air

ℹ tourist information

♿ facilities for visitors with disabilities

✋ admission charge

↔ other places of interest near by

❓ other practical information

➤ indicates the page where you will find a fuller description

This book is divided into five sections to cover the most important aspects of your visit to Mallorca.

Viewing Mallorca pages 5–14
An introduction to Mallorca by the author.
Mallorca's Features
Essence of Mallorca
The Shaping of Mallorca
Peace and Quiet
Mallorca's Famous

Top Ten pages 15–26
The author's choice of the Top Ten places to visit in Mallorca, with practical information.

What to See pages 27–90
Alphabetical listings of the main attractions in Palma and around the island.
Practical information
Snippets of 'Did You Know…' information
4 suggested walks
4 suggested tours
2 features

Where To... pages 91–116
Detailed listings of the best places to eat, stay, shop, take the children and be entertained.

Practical Matters pages 117–24
A highly visual section containing essential travel information.

Maps
All map references are to the individual maps in the What to See section of this guide. For example, La Seu in Palma has the reference ✚ 34B2 – indicating the page on which the map is located and the grid square in which the cathedral is to be found. A list of the maps that have been used in this travel guide can be found in the index. As with the maps, place names in the text are given in Catalan; where a Spanish word or phrase is more widely used, that is given instead.

Prices
Where appropriate, an indication of the cost of an establishment is given by £ signs: **£££** denotes higher prices, **££** denotes average prices, while **£** denotes lower charges.

Star Ratings
Most of the places described in this book have been given a separate rating:
😊😊😊   Do not miss
😊😊   Highly recommended
😊   Worth seeing

Viewing
Mallorca

Above: *Green shutters,
Cala Santanyí;*
Right: *Old timer in local
café in Muro*

Tony Kelly's Mallorca

Mallorca or Majorca?
Are they the same place or not? Yes and no. Majorca, with a hard 'j', is a place invented by foreigners, where the sun always shines, the beer flows and the nearest you get to local culture is an argument with a taxi-driver. Mallorca, the local name for the island, is somewhere quite different and far more complex. This book is about Mallorca.

Sheep with bells around their necks grazing beneath olive trees; hilltop sanctuaries where you spend the night in what was once a monk's cell. These are probably not your typical images of Mallorca.

If you thought Mallorca was all sweaty bodies, in the disco and on the beach, think again. It is that, of course – that's the main reason why 8 million tourists visit the island every year. But there is an awful lot more to Mallorca than sun, sea and sand.

Whisper it gently, but Mallorca is changing its image. Fed up with being labelled cheap and cheerful, it has gone for a new approach. High-rise apartment blocks are being torn down, to be replaced by tree-lined promenades. Manor houses and country estates are being converted into stylish hotels. Tourists are encouraged to come in winter, to walk, cycle and play golf. The island that led the way into mass tourism is now leading the way out.

Not just sand and sea – Mallorca is starting to attract walkers and cyclists

For such a small island, the variations are extraordinary. You can spend one day lying on the beach, the next walking in the mountains. Castles, caves, countryside, hidden coves... whatever you want from a holiday, it is probably there. Except, perhaps, snow.

Of course there is nowhere in Mallorca still waiting to be 'discovered' – even the tiniest villages are heavily dependent on tourism. But strike off the main roads and into the small towns on the plain, simply go wherever you see a cluster of brown houses on a hill, and you will find a Mallorca utterly at odds with the familiar image.

Mallorca's Features

Geography
• Mallorca is the largest of the Balearic islands, a group that includes Menorca, Ibiza and Formentera.
• Mallorca measures 100km from east to west and 75km from north to south.
• Mallorca lies 200km south of Barcelona off the east coast of Spain.
• Mallorca has 555km of coastline and 80 beaches.
• The rocky islands Cabrera and Sa Dragonera provide havens for nesting seabirds.
• The Serra de Tramuntana and Serra de Llevant are two mountain ranges divided by a fertile central plain.
• Palma has an average daily maximum temperature of 21.4°C and an average of seven hours of sunshine per day throughout the year.

Pine-clad cliffs lean into the sea along the spectacular north coast

Tourism
• Mallorca received 1 million tourists in 1966, 3 million in 1978 and 8 million in 2000, of whom 41% were from Germany, 26% from Britain and 12% from Spain.
• On busy days in summer up to 700 flights land at Palma airport, carrying up to 100,000 passengers.
• Mallorca has 200,000 hotel beds and 60,000 in tourist apartments.
• Mallorca has enough restaurant tables for a quarter of the population to eat out every night.
• Mallorca's GDP (Gross Domestic Product) per capita is more than 50% above the Spanish average. Two thirds of the population work in tourism, which represents about 60% of GDP.

Language
• The official languages are Catalan and Castilian Spanish, though Catalan has enjoyed a strong revival in recent years and is now the preferred language in education and local government.
• Most people speak Mallorquín, a dialect of Catalan.

People
Of 630,000 people in Mallorca, half live in the capital Palma. The next biggest towns are Manacor (30,000) and Inca (22,000). The population has doubled since 1950 and includes a large number of expatriates – around 30,000 Germans and almost as many British.

Essence of Mallorca

Mallorca's character is shaped, above all, by its climate. The people of the Mediterranean know how to take life slowly – they still have time to sit in the shade and chat, to take a siesta rather than rushing back to work, to enjoy the outdoors whether it is the mountains or the sea.

The warm climate has long attracted outsiders, whose influence can still be felt; Romans, Arabs and Europeans have all left their mark on Mallorca's landscape and culture. But what have not changed are the enduring values of an island people, courteous, proud and self-sufficient.

Aquarium at Porto Cristo (above); fisherman at Port de Sóller (below); the dubious attractions of Platja de Palma (right)

THE **10** ESSENTIALS

If you only have a short time to visit Mallorca, or would like to get a real flavour of the island, here are the essentials:

• **Spend a day in Palma** exploring the old city, then join the evening *passeig* along the waterfront for a drink in one of the island's trendiest bars (➤ 30–40).

• **Take the joyride to Sóller** on a vintage electric train through the mountains (➤ 71).

• **Enjoy a boat trip** around the coast, passing hidden coves which you cannot reach in a car.

• **Walk in the Serra de Tramuntana** (➤ 83–4), breathing in the heady mix of fresh air, sea breeze and scented wild herbs.

• **Sit at a quayside restaurant** eating fresh fish – choose from any one of the island's ports (➤ 92–9).

Take the tram to Port de Sóller and the boat to Sa Calobra – or spend the day working on your tan

• **Visit the monastery at Valldemossa** where Chopin and George Sand spent the winter of 1838–39 (➤ 26).

• **Drive (or walk) to a hilltop sanctuary** to experience 'the other Mallorca' – if you really want to get away from it all, spend the night.

• **Visit the traditional market at Sineu** (➤ 86) to haggle over everything from sausages to sheep.

• **Brave the crowds on a resort beach** – you haven't 'done' Mallorca until you have.

• **Find out where there is a local festival going on** (➤ 116) – and drop everything to get there.

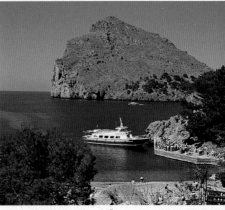

The Shaping of Mallorca

5000 BC
Evidence of human habitation in caves on the north coast.

1300–800 BC
The Talaiotic culture creates settlements like those at Artà and Capocorb Vell.

400 BC
First references to *honderos* (Balearic slingers) fighting in the Punic Wars.

123 BC
The island is conquered by the Romans, who name it Balearis Major, introduce vineyards and olives, and establish their capital at Pollentia, now Alcúdia.

AD 426
Vandal invasion leads to the persecution of Christians.

534
Byzantine conquest restores Christianity and brings Mallorca into the province of Sardinia.

902
Arab invasion – Mallorca enters the Caliphate of Córdoba. Oranges and almonds are introduced, along with windmills and irrigation techniques. Palma, known as Medina Mayurqa, is the envy of Europe, with street lights and heated baths.

1229
The origins of modern Mallorca – the conquest by Jaume I of Aragón. Catalan becomes the main language.

1275
Ramón Llull establishes his first hermitage at Puig de Randa.

1276
On Jaume I's death, his kingdom is divided up and his son Jaume II becomes the first King of Mallorca.

1276–1349
The 'Golden Age of Independence' – the building of Castell de Bellver, Palau de l'Almudaina and Alcúdia's city walls.

1349
Jaume III is killed at Llucmajor and Mallorca's independence ends when the island is reincorporated into Aragón.

1492
Modern Spain is created with the union of Aragón, Castile and Granada.

16th–18th Centuries
Repeated pirate attacks lead to the building of watchtowers around the coast.

1715
After victory in the War of the Spanish Succession, Felipe V imposes central rule and the Castilian language on the island of Mallorca.

Statue of Ramón Llull on the waterfront at Palma

10

1836
Opening of a steamer service between Mallorca and Spain.

1879–98
Period of 'gold fever' due to the booming export trade in wine and almonds – until the vines are destroyed by the phylloxera virus, leading to mass emigration.

1902–3
The Gran Hotel opens in Palma. Thomas Cook runs its first tours to Mallorca.

1905
Founding of the Fomento del Turismo de Mallorca (tourist board).

1929
Opening of the Hotel Formentor.

1936–39
The Spanish Civil War, followed by dictatorship under General Franco.

1950
The first charter flight lands in Mallorca.

1960
The opening of Son Sant Joan airport leads to the start of the tourist boom.

1966
Mallorca receives one million tourists.

The Spanish Civil War led to repression throughout Spain

1975
Death of Franco and restoration of the monarchy.

1978
A new constitution grants limited autonomy to the Spanish regions.

1983
The Balearic Islands become an autonomous region with their capital at Palma. Catalan becomes the official language.

1984
Opening of La Residencia hotel in Deià.

1986
Spain joins the European Community.

1988
A new coastal law prohibits further development within 100m of the sea.

12
... new terminal at Son Sant Joan airport is launched, increasing capacity to 27 million passengers a year.

2002
Euro banknotes and coins are introduced across Spain.

Peace & Quiet

If you want peace and quiet in Mallorca, go in winter – only 10 per cent of foreign tourists visit between November and March. The island is particularly beautiful in February, when almond blossom carpets the ground like snow. Even in the height of summer, there are plenty of opportunities to escape the crowds. Half of the locals live in Palma, and 90 per cent of the tourists stay on a few small stretches of coast – which leaves large areas of Mallorca just waiting to be explored.

Olive trees near Andratx – it is still surprisingly easy to get away from it all in Mallorca

Rights of Way
Walkers have the right of way on all coastal paths, plus routes to miradors, monasteries and mountain peaks (except Puig Major). In recent years, many landowners have attempted to deny access by erecting 'private' signs. If challenged, just state clearly where you are going.

Walking

The obvious areas are the mountains, especially the Serra de Tramuntana (▶ 83–84). At the lower levels, up to around 700m, you walk through *garrigue*, a typical Mediterranean landscape where Aleppo pines mix with wild olives and the stony ground sprouts beautiful wild flowers – orchids and peonies and cistus and asphodel – in spring. (Spring here arrives early, from late February through to May.) Higher up, you reach the *maquis* scrubland, where little grows apart from thorny bushes of heather, bracken, rosemary and broom. Above 1,000m the land is barren – but the views from this height are magnificent and the sense of isolation complete.

Take sensible precautions when walking in the mountains – good boots, extra clothing, food and water, a map, compass and whistle. If you prefer more gentle walks, just strike out along any of the minor roads between the small towns on the plain, or follow a coastal footpath to find your own private bay.

Birds

Mallorca is a paradise for birdwatchers, who come from all over Europe each spring and autumn to see migrating birds on their way to and from wintering in Africa. The best times are April to May and September to October, and the best areas are S'Albufera (▶ 77) and the Salines de Llevant near Ses Salines (▶ 85). The reedbeds of S'Albufera come alive each spring with the song of herons and warblers; other species include egrets, terns, hoopoes, sandpipers and woodcat shrike. Numerous wading birds and wildfowl are attracted to the salt marshes at Ses Salines, including plovers, stilts, water rails and black-tailed godwits. Good spots for watching seabirds include Cap de Ses Salines on the south coast and Cap de Formentor in the northeast (▶ 18), where shags and shearwaters nestle on the cliffs.

Birds of Prey

The mountains of the Serra de Tramuntana are a haven for birds of prey, including ospreys, peregrines, Montagu's harriers and Eleanora's falcons. Rarest of all are the black vultures, of which only a few dozen remain in the area around Lluc monastery. An exhibition at the monastery describes a conservation programme to protect both these and another endangered species, the Mallorcan midwife toad. The best places to see black vultures, and other predatory birds, are at the Cúber and Gorg Blau reservoirs on the road through the mountains from Lluc to Sóller.

The mountain ranges of Mallorca are one of the last remaining European habitats of the black vulture

13

Mallorca's Famous

Michael Douglas (1944–)
The American actor Michael Douglas is a frequent visitor to Mallorca, where he has a home overlooking the north coast. His passion for Mallorca is reflected in his Costa Nord cultural centre (► 51) in Valldemossa. In 1999 he was awarded the *silver siurell* by the government of Mallorca for his role in promoting the island.

Ramón Llull

Ramón Llull (1235–1316) was a wealthy courtier in Palma until a disastrous seduction attempt (► 75) led him to retire to Puig de Randa in isolation. Devoting himself to prayer and study, he wrote in Catalan and Latin on everything from algebra to metaphysics; he is widely seen as the father of the Catalan language. Recalled to the court by Jaume II, he established an Oriental language school at Valldemossa and learnt Arabic with the help of a Moorish slave. He was stoned to death attempting to convert Muslims in Tunisia.

Junípero Serra

The Mallorcan missionary Junípero Serra (1713–84) is honoured in the Capitol in Washington as 'the founder of California'. Of course California was there already; but it was Serra, sent there at the age of 54 after 14 years in Mexico, who established the missions which have grown into some of America's biggest cities, including San Diego and San Francisco. A museum in his home town of Petra (► 64) tells the story. He was beatified in 1988, the first step on the road to sainthood.

Joan Miró

Though not strictly Mallorcan, Joan Miró (1893–1983), the Catalan artist, spent the last 27 years of his life in Mallorca and the islanders have adopted him as their own. His bright, surreal designs adorn everything from tourist posters (the widely used España and Mallorca logos are his) to T-shirts and the mural in the Parc de la Mar in Palma. His house and studio near Palma have been turned into a gallery of his work (► 56).

Statue of Junípero Serra in Palma (above); Joan Miró at work (right)

Top Ten

Above: *Narrow streets of Valldemossa;*
Right: *Detail on Portal del Mirador, La Seu*

1
Alcúdia

🕂 29D5

🍴 Choice of restaurants and bars (£–££)

🚌 From Palma/Port d'Alcúdia

↔ Port d'Alcúdia (▶ 67)

❓ Market held Tue, Sun

Ciutat Romà

🕐 Tue–Fri 10–1:15, 3:30–5:15, Sat–Sun 10–1:15

✋ Cheap

Museu Monogràfic de Pollentia

✉ Carrer Sant Jaume 30

☎ 971 547004

🕐 Tue–Fri 10–1:30, 3:30–5:30, Sat–Sun 10:30–1

✋ Cheap

Portal del Moll leads directly into the heart of the city

A perfectly restored walled city on the site of a Roman settlement, with remains of Roman houses and an amphitheatre.

Not to be confused with the holiday resort of the same name, which is actually down at Port d'Alcúdia (▶ 67), the old town is a gem of a place, a maze of narrow streets enclosed by carefully restored medieval ramparts. There were Phoenician and Greek settlements here, but the town reached its heyday in the 2nd century BC, when the Roman invaders made it their capital, Pollentia ('power'). Destroyed by Vandals in the 6th century, the town returned to greatness under the Moors, who built *al-kudia* ('the town on the hill'). The walls you see today were added after the Spanish conquest in the 14th century.

You enter the city through one of the two town gates – the Portal del Moll, with two square towers and two massive palm trees standing guard, is the symbol of Alcúdia. The narrow streets of the old town, especially Carrer d'en Serra, are resonant of Palma's Arab quarter.

A short walk from the parish church of Sant Jaume takes you to three interesting sights, connected by signposted footpaths. Closest to town are the remains of Roman houses at Pollentia, **Ciutat Romà**; near here are the well-preserved Teatre Romà (Roman amphitheatre) and the Oratori de Santa Anna, one of Mallorca's oldest churches. After exploring the Roman remains, interpret them at the **Museu Monogràfic de Pollentia** beside the parish church.

2
Badia de Palma
(Palma Bay)

*The good, the bad and the ugly sides
of Mallorca's tourist development meet along
a 25-km stretch of coast.*

28B3

Numerous bars and
restaurants in all the
resorts (£)

From Palma to all the
resorts

The former villages of S'Arenal and Magaluf sit facing each
other across Palma Bay. Once upon a time, a fisherman
casting his net into the sea at S'Arenal could have

gazed around an empty
coastline where the only
buildings to stand out
would have been Palma's
cathedral and castle.
Nowadays he would
barely be able to distin-
guish them among a
continuous stretch of
hotels, a concrete jungle
extending all the way to
Magaluf. And he wouldn't
be there anyway as there
are few fish left to catch.

Like it or loathe it, you
are bound to spend some
time in Palma Bay – even
if you are not staying
here, you should visit at
least once to see some
of the best, and the
worst, that Mallorca has
to offer. Each of the
resorts (described separately in the What To See section)
has its own character – young or old, British or German,
cheap and cheerful or jet-set rich. One moment you can
be in Portals Nous, with its chic marina crammed with
millionaires' yachts (you have to be seriously rich just to
look at the restaurant menus here), the next in seedy
Magaluf, all British pubs and wet T-shirt contests.

Occasionally you come across a glimpse of what this
coastline must once have been like. Follow the road
beyond Magaluf through the pine woods. Suddenly you
are among tiny coves where, out of season, you might still
find your own private beach. Eventually you reach the
headland of Cap de Cala Figuera where you can look back
at sweeping views of the entire bay. Cliffs plunge into the
clear blue sea, with not a hotel in sight. Come up here at
midnight for utter peace and solitude; but listen carefully
and you might just be able to hear the disco beat of
Magaluf pounding away beneath you.

Boat tours of Palma Bay
in summer from Palma,
S'Arenal, Palma Nova
and Magaluf

Level beach
promenades at Platja de
Palma and Magaluf

Magaluf (▶ 59), Palma
Nova (▶ 63), Platja de
Palma (▶ 64), Portals
Nous (▶ 72), Portals
Vells (▶ 72), Ses Illetes
(▶ 85)

*Sun, sea and sand but
little solitude – resorts like
Magaluf epitomise the
growth of Mallorcan
tourism*

17

3
Cap de Formentor

🕂 29E5

🍴 Café with snacks at Cap de Formentor (£); restaurant (£££) in Hotel Formentor

🚌 From Palma and Port de Pollença in summer

🛥 From Port de Pollença to Formentor beach and Cap de Formentor in summer

❓ The best time to see birds and flowers is spring

There are several opportunities to stop and admire the view along the twisting road to Cap de Formentor

This wild peninsula on Mallorca's northeast tip has stunning views, sandy beaches and the island's original luxury hotel.

The 20-km drive from Port de Pollença to Mallorca's most northerly point has scenery as dramatic as anyone could wish for. Cliffs 400m tall jut into the sea, their weird rock formations attracting nesting seabirds, while pine trees seem to grow out of the rocks. The drive is also famously scary – a local legend has it that the parish priest and the local bus driver arrived at the Pearly Gates, and only the driver was admitted to heaven. The reason? He had led far more people to pray.

Six kilometres from Port de Pollença you reach the Mirador des Colomer – scramble up the steps for views over a rocky islet. A path opposite the steps leads to an old watchtower from which you can see the whole of the peninsula as well as the bays of Pollença and Alcúdia. The road continues through pine woods and past more *miradors* (each one helpfully indicated with a picture of an old-fashioned camera) before tunnelling through En Fumat mountain, where you look down over Mallorca's most inaccessible beach. Eventually you reach a lighthouse with the inevitable bar and shop and more stunning views, all the way to Menorca on a good day.

On the way back, stop at Formentor beach and the Hotel Formentor, which opened in 1929 and has been pampering the rich and famous ever since. The fine sandy beach used to be reserved for the hotel's guests, but democracy has opened it to the masses.

4
Castell d'Alaró

A popular walk to a ruined castle and hilltop chapel offering spectacular views all the way to the sea.

A castle has stood on this site since Moorish times; it was so impregnable that the Arab commander was able to hold out for two years after the Christian conquest. Later, in 1285, two heroes of Mallorcan independence, Cabrit and Brassa, defended the castle against Alfonsó III of Aragón and were burned alive on a spit when he finally took it by storm. Their punishment was a consequence of their impudent defiance of the king. They pretended to confuse Alfonso's name with that of a local fish – *anfós*, shouting: 'We like our *anfós* grilled.' The present ruins date from the 15th century and seem almost to grow out of the rock, dominating the landscape for miles around.

The climb up here is one of Mallorca's most popular walks, especially on Sundays. From the town of Alaró it is a stiff climb of about two hours, following the signs from the PM210 to Orient; you can also leave from Orient (► 63), following a small path opposite L'Hermitage hotel, again taking around two hours in total. The paths converge above Es Verger restaurant (you can even bring a car this far if you don't mind the potholes and the hairpin bends), where you can fill up with roast lamb to fortify you for the final steep climb.

At last you reach the castle, 800m above sea level; look back at the view, stretching across the entire plain to Palma and out to sea. A few minutes further brings you to the summit, with a small chapel and sanctuary, and (bliss!) a restaurant and bar. If you are inspired by the views, you can stay the night here in one of the simple rooms.

✚ 28C4

☎ Sanctuary: 971 510480

🕐 Open access

🍴 Es Verger (££) on the way up; simple restaurant (££) at the sanctuary

🚌 From Palma to Alaró

↔ Orient (► 63)

The final steps of the climb – almost time for a well-earned drink at the hilltop bar

5
Castell de Bellver

28B3

Parc Bellver

971 730657

Apr–Sep, Mon–Sat
8–8:30; Oct–Mar,
Mon–Sat 8–7:15

3 or 21 to Plaça Gomila

Cheap. Free entrance
on Sun, when museum
closed

Evening concerts in Jul,
Aug

*A well-preserved 14th-century royal fortress with
fragrant pine woods, an interesting museum and
superb views over Palma Bay.*

Looking up at this castle, so perfectly maintained, it is hard
to believe that it has been standing for almost 700 years.
Begun by Jaume II in 1300 and built by Pere Salvà, the
architect of the Almudaina Palace, it is unique among
Spanish castles in being entirely round. Three large towers
surround a central courtyard, connected by an arch to a
free-standing keep. The courtyard itself is on two levels,
the ground floor with semicircular arches and a flat roof,
the upper level with Gothic arches and rib vaulting. For the
full effect, walk around the moat then climb onto the roof
and look down into the courtyard to compare the
contrasting styles. While you are there, look out over the
city and the bay for one of the best views in Palma (Bellver
means 'lovely view' in Catalan).

*Bellver Castle has been
both a royal residence
and a military prison, but
its main function now is
as a historical museum*

For many centuries the castle was used as a prison;
Jaume III's widow and sons were imprisoned here for
most of their lives. These days it contains Palma's
museum of municipal history which traces the development of the city through its artefacts, with pottery from
Talaiotic, Roman, Arab and Spanish periods.

You can get there by car or taxi, or take a bus to Plaça
Gomila and climb up through the pine woods above Carrer
de Bellver, passing a chapel on the way.

6
Coves d'Artà

A fascinating network of underground caverns, whose weird stalactites and stalagmites conjure up mysterious images of Heaven and Hell.

If you only have time to visit one set of caves on the east coast, this is the one to see. Now that they are a sanitised tourist attraction, it is hard to imagine how French geologist Édouard Martel felt when he first stepped into these caves, dark, mysterious and terrifying, in 1876. In fact they had been known about for centuries – Jaume I found 2,000 Arabs hiding here with their cattle during the Christian conquest and they were later used by hermits, pirates and smugglers – but it was Martel who first studied and chronicled these grottoes, 46m above the sea at Cap Vermell, at the instigation of Archduke Ludwig Salvator. Another early visitor was Jules Verne; the caves are said to have inspired his *Journey to the Centre of the Earth*.

Back into daylight as you emerge from the caves

The guided tour comes with special effects and the various chambers are given Dantesque names – Hell, Purgatory, Paradise. The descent into Hell is swiftly followed by a *son et lumière* display. Stalactites point down from the mouldy roof like daggers, somehow defying gravity. One of the chambers is as large as the nave of Palma Cathedral, and the Queen of Pillars, a stalagmite 22m tall, could almost be a Gothic column. It is growing upwards at the rate of 2cm every 100 years; in another 5,000 years or so it will be joined to the ceiling.

You emerge from the caves to a view of the sea, framed by the cavern entrance. Disabled visitors and others with limited mobility will find the staircases in here particularly difficult. All visitors should be sensibly shod, as the floor can be slippery.

 29F4

 971 841293

Jul–Sep, daily 10–7; Oct–Jun, daily 10–5

 Bars at Platja de Canyamel near by (£)

From Artà and Cala Rajada in summer

 None

 Moderate

7
Deià

An idyllic village of green-shuttered, ochre-coloured houses has become a millionaires' hideaway in the shadow of the Teix mountain.

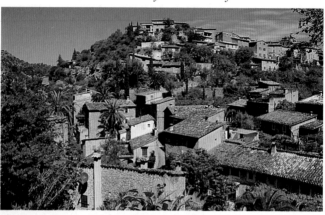

✚ 28B4

🍴 Wide choice of restaurants and bars (£–£££)

🚌 From Palma, Valldemossa and Port de Sóller

↔ Lluc-Alcari (► 58), Son Marroig (► 88)

❓ Classical music festival Aug–Sep

Deià could have been just another pretty Mallorcan village had Robert Graves not decided to make it his home. The English poet and novelist first moved here in 1932 with his mistress Laura Riding and returned in 1946 with his second wife. Muses followed, friends came to stay, and before long Deià had established a reputation as a foreign artists' colony. Now it is on every tourist itinerary as the prime example of 'the other Mallorca' and this small village contains two luxury hotels. Rich foreign residents, like the actor Michael Douglas, are apt to bemoan the arrival of tour buses; the few locals who remain are philosophical about outsiders.

Graves was hardly the first to discover Deià. An 1878 guidebook noted its 'collection of strange and eccentric foreigners' and it has stayed that way ever since. Climb the Carrer es Puig, Deià's only real street, passing ceramic Stations of the Cross, to reach the parish church and the small cemetery where Graves is buried. His tombstone, like many others, is inscribed in simple handwriting set into the drying concrete – *Robert Graves, Poeta, 1895–1985*. If you want to know more, read *Wild Olives – Life in Majorca with Robert Graves* by his son William Graves.

From Deià you can scramble down to Cala de Deià, a small shingle beach set in an attractive cove, where local artists still continue the Graves tradition of naked swimming and long parties at weekends.

Deià is a lot more cosmopolitan than it looks

8
Lluc

*Mallorca's most sacred site –
a former monastery in a spectacular setting in the
Serra de Tramuntana.*

Lluc has been a centre of pilgrimage since the 13th century when an Arab shepherd boy, newly converted to Christianity, discovered a dark wooden statue of the Virgin in a cleft in the rock. The image was placed in the local church but three times it returned miraculously to its cave, whereupon the villagers recognised a message from God and built a chapel to house it.

La Moreneta ('the Little Dark One') is now encrusted with precious stones, and sits in a chapel decorated with the arms of every Mallorcan town. Pilgrims and tourists queue to pay homage, especially on Sundays and at 11AM before the daily concerts by Els Blauets choir. The choir, named after their blue cassocks, was established in 1531, comprising 40 boys, 'natives of Mallorca, of pure blood, sound in grammar and song'. The service is marred by the whirring and flashing of cameras, and if it's meditation you seek, come back instead for the evening Mass.

➕ 28C5

☎ 971 871525

🕐 Museum: daily 10–5:30; Monastery: daily 9–8:30

🍴 Sa Fonda (££) in the former monks' refectory

🚌 Two buses daily from Palma and Inca

✋ Monastery: free; Museum: cheap

❓ Choir concert daily 11:15 followed by Mass at 11:30; second service at dusk open to those staying; annual night-time pilgrimage from Palma to Lluc on foot (48km) – usually held in first week of Aug

The monastery complex includes Els Porxerets, the former pilgrims' quarters with stabling beneath the rooms, and the Way of the Rosary, with touches by Antoni Gaudí. From the hilltop cross you look down over an unexpected farmland valley and up into the pine-covered mountains. You can stay at Lluc but it is more like a hotel than a hermitage – the 100 'cells' have *en suite* bathrooms and there are several restaurants and bars. There is also a **museum** – among the displays of ceramics, chalices and coins is a collection of paintings by the 20th-century Mallorcan artist Josep Coll Bardolet, with scenes from Deià, Valldemossa and Fornalutx.

*The chapel at Lluc is
dedicated to the Virgin Mary*

9
La Seu (Palma Cathedral)

The glory of Palma – a magnificent Gothic cathedral whose sandstone walls and flying buttresses seem to rise out of the sea.

Anything you see inside Palma cathedral will come as a disappointment once you have stood on the seafront and gazed up at its golden sandstone exterior, climbing above the old city walls. La Seu stands out utterly from its surroundings, a demonstration of the might of Mallorca's Christian conquerors to all who arrived by sea.

Tradition has it that a storm arose as Jaume I was sailing towards Mallorca. He vowed that if he landed safely he would build a great church in honour of the Virgin. On New Year's Day 1230, a day after the fall of Palma, the foundation stone was symbolically laid on the site of the

city's main mosque. Work continued for 400 years – and had to resume in 1851 when an earthquake destroyed the west front. More touches were added in the 20th century by the Catalan architect Antoni Gaudí.

You enter through a side door, passing a small museum; head for the west portal and gaze down the long nave. Light pours in through the rose window, one of the world's largest, 12m across and studded with 1,236 pieces of stained glass. The columns are ringed with wrought-iron candelabra by Gaudí; his most controversial addition is the unfinished Crown of Thorns, fashioned from cardboard and cork and suspended above the altar.

Be sure to walk around to the south front, facing the sea, to look at the Portal del Mirador, a 15th-century door by Guillem Sagrera featuring scenes from the Last Supper.

 34B2

✉ Plaça d'Almoina

☎ 971 723130

🕐 Apr–Oct, Mon–Fri 10–6, Sat 10–2; Nov–Mar, Mon–Fri 10–3, Sat 10–2

♿ Few

💷 Cheap (free for services)

↔ Museu Diocesà (▶ 37), Palau de l'Almudaina (▶ 38)

❓ High Mass, Sun 10:30

Even the royal palace is cut down to size by the mystery of Palma cathedral, standing out above its surroundings on the waterfront

25

10
Valldemossa

✚ 28B4

🍴 Choice of restaurants and bars (££)

🚌 From Palma, Deià and Port de Sóller

❓ Regular Chopin piano concerts in Palau del Rei Sanç (entered on same ticket as monastery); La Beata procession in honour of Santa Catalina Thomás, 27–28 Jul; Chopin Festival in Aug; market held Sun

Reial Cartoixa

☎ 971 612106

🕐 Mar–Oct, Mon–Sat 9:30–6, Sun 10–1; Nov–Feb, Mon–Sat 9:30–4:30, Sun 10–1

✋ Expensive

The small town in the mountains where Mallorcan tourism began one cold, damp winter in 1838.

Try as it might – and it doesn't try very hard – Valldemossa cannot escape its connection with Frédéric Chopin and his lover George Sand. They arrived in 1838, having rented a former monk's cell, planning to carry on their affair away from the gossip of Paris and hoping that the climate would benefit Chopin's health (he had tuberculosis). Nothing worked out as planned. The weather was wet and windy, the couple were shunned by the locals, Chopin's piano failed to arrive and the relationship never recovered. Sand took out her anger on Valldemossa in a spiteful book, *Winter in Majorca*, which the locals, labelled as thieves and savages, still gleefully sell to visitors.

The **Reial Cartoixa** (Royal Carthusian Monastery) is the focus of any visit – white-arched corridors lead to 'cells' containing museums on various themes. Visit the old pharmacy – you can almost smell the herbs – then look into the library, where the monks would meet for half an hour a week, their only human contact. There is a fine modern art museum, with works by Picasso, Miró and Juli Ramis, and of course there is Chopin's cell...

Most people come for the Chopin experience, but there is more to Valldemossa than that. It is also the birthplace of Catalina Thomás, Mallorca's patron saint. A peasant girl born in 1531, she became a nun in Palma and was renowned for her humility. Almost every home in Valldemossa has a plaque imploring her prayers, and her birthplace at Carrer Rectoría 5 has been turned into a shrine. She would probably be appalled.

The newest attraction in Valldemossa is Michael Douglas' Costa Nord (▶ 51).

The Carthusian monastery stands at the centre of the highest town in Mallorca

What To See

Above: Hairpin bends on the way down to Sa Calobra;
Right: Monument, Santa Ponça

MALLORCA

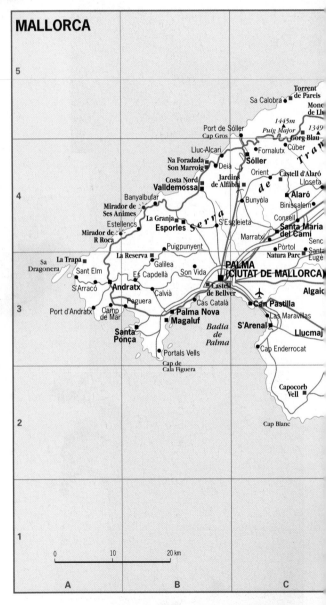

5

Torrent
de Pareis
Sa Calobra
Mone
de Ll
1445m
Port de Sóller
Puig Major
1349
Cap Gros
Gorg Blau
Lluc-Alcari
Fornalutx
Cúber
Na Foradada
Deià
Sóller
Son Marroig
Orient
Castell d'Alaró
Costa Nord
Jardins
Lloseta
Valldemossa
de Alfàbia
Alaró
4
Banyalbufar
Bunyola
Binissalem
Mirador de
Ses Animes
La Granja
Consell
Estellencs
S'Esgleieta
Santa Maria
Mirador de
Esporles
Serra
del Camí
R Roca
Marratxí
Senc
Puigpunyent
Pòrtol
Santa
La Reserva
Natura Parc
Euge
Sa
La Trapa
Galilea
PALMA
Dragonera
Sant Elm
Es Capdellà
Son Vida
(CIUTAT DE MALLORCA)
S'Arracó
Andratx
Castell
Algaic
Calvià
de Bellver
3
Port d'Andratx
Peguera
Càs Català
Can Pastilla
Camp
Palma Nova
Las Maravillas
de Mar
Magaluf
S'Arenal
Llucmaj
Santa
Badia
Ponça
de
Portals Vells
Palma
Cap Enderrocat
Cap de
Cala Figuera

Capocorb
Vell
2
Cap Blanc

1

0   10   20 km

A   B   C

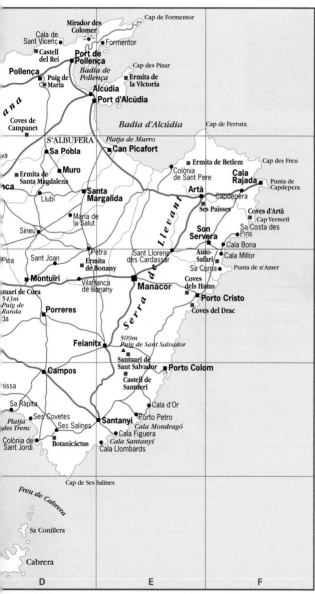

Cap de Formentor

Mirador des Colomer

Cala de Sant Vicenç

Formentor

Castell del Rei

Port de Pollença

Cap des Pinar

Pollença

Badia de Pollença

Ermita de la Victoria

Puig de Maria

Alcúdia

Port d'Alcúdia

ana

Coves de Campanet

Badia d'Alcúdia

Cap de Ferrutx

S'ALBUFERA

Platja de Murro

Sa Pobla

Can Picafort

Ermita de Santa Magdalena

Muro

Ermita de Betlem

Cap des Freu

ca

Colònia de Sant Pere

Cala Rajada

Llubí

Santa Margalida

Artà

Punta de Capdepera

Sineu

Maria de la Salut

Capdepera

Ses Païsses

Coves d'Artà

Cap Vermell

Son Servera

Sa Costa des Pins

Pina

Sant Joan

Petra

Sant Llorenç des Cardassar

Cala Bona

Auto-Safari

Cala Millor

Ermita de Bonany

Sa Coma

Punta de n'Amer

Montuïri

Vilafranca de Bonany

Manacor

Coves dels Hams

Serra de Llevant

tuari de Cura
543m
Puig de Randa
da

Porreres

Porto Cristo

Coves del Drac

Felanitx

509m
Puig de Sant Salvador

Santuari de Sant Salvador

Porto Colom

Campos

Castell de Santueri

hissa

Sa Rápita

Cala d'Or

Platja des Trenc

Ses Covetes

Ses Salines

Santanyí

Porto Petro

Cala Mondragó

Cala Figuera

Colònia de Sant Jordi

Botanicáctus

Cala Santanyí

Cala Llombards

Cap de Ses Salines

Freu de Cabrera

Sa Conillera

Cabrera

D   E   F

Palma

Palma comes as a surprise to many people – it is stylish, sophisticated, intimate yet bursting with life. Half of Mallorca's population live here, enjoying the island's best restaurants, shops and nightlife as well as a thriving arts scene and a lively café society.

Palma's masterpiece is its Gothic cathedral, rising out of the city walls which once marked the edge of the sea. Close to here is the old Arab quarter, its maze of narrow streets hiding museums, palaces and exquisite courtyards. But do not explore old Palma at the expense of its modern side. Take coffee in the former Gran Hotel, visit an art gallery in a converted mansion, join Palma's bright young things on their evening *passeig* along the waterfront, and you will begin to appreciate the variety of this fascinating city.

> '*The time will doubtless come when frail dilettantes, and even lovely women, will be able to visit Palma with no more exhaustion and discomfort than Geneva.*'

GEORGE SAND
Winter in Majorca (1855), translated
by Robert Graves (1956)

Palma

Known to the Arabs as Medina Mayurqa and to Mallorcans simply as *Ciutat* (City), Palma is in fact named after the Roman city of Palmaria. Here you can almost literally uncover the different layers of Mallorcan history. The Roman city still exists, a metre or two beneath the ground; inhabitants of houses near the cathedral are still discovering Roman remains. The cathedral was built on the site of a mosque, once a Roman temple; the royal palace replaced an Arab *alcázar*.

The city you see today, however, is a relatively recent creation. The tree-lined promenades of La Rambla and Passeig des Born, home to florists and newspaper sellers, were built in the 19th century on a dried-up river bed. The walls which once surrounded the city were pulled down to create the ring road Las Avingudas, and Passeig Marítim, the waterfront highway and promenade, was only reclaimed from the sea in the 1950s.

Palma's pedestrian shopping streets seem designed for browsing – but everything stops during the afternoon siesta

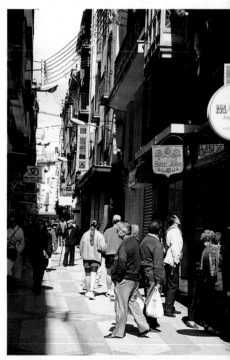

Most of the main sights are located within the area bounded by the old walls, especially to the north and east of the cathedral. Wander along any alley in the ancient Arab quarter, peering through wrought-iron gates and heavy wooden doors, and you will be rewarded with glimpses of one magnificent patio after another, with their stone staircases, galleries and arcades.

But you have not truly seen Palma until you have surveyed it from the water-front, with the cathedral and Almudaina palace rising proudly above the defensive walls of the old city, their golden sandstone lit up by the afternoon sun.

What to See in Palma

BANYS ÀRABS (ARAB BATHS)   ✪✪

⊞ 35C1
✉ Carrer Can Serra 7
☎ 971 721549
🕐 Daily 9–8
🍴 Bar Sa Murada near by (£)
♿ None
💷 Cheap
↔ Museu de Mallorca
   (▶ 37)

These 10th-century baths are virtually all that remain of the Arab city of Medina Mayurqa. They were probably part of a nobleman's house and are similar to those found in other Islamic cities. The *tepidarium* has a dome in the shape of a half-orange, with 25 round shafts for sunlight, supported by a dozen columns. Notice how each of the columns is different – they were probably salvaged from the ruins of various Roman buildings, an early example of recycling. *Hammams* were meeting places as well as wash-houses, and the courtyard with its cactus, palm and orange trees would have made a pleasant place to cool off after a hot bath.

BASÍLICA DE SANT FRANCESC   ✪✪

⊞ 35C2
✉ Plaça Sant Francesc
☎ 971 712695
🕐 Mon–Sat 9:30–12:30,
   3:30–6, Sun 9:30–12:30
💷 Cheap

The façade of this 13th-century church (remodelled after it was struck by lightning in the 17th century) is typically Mallorcan – a massive, forbidding sandstone wall with a delicately carved portal and a rose window at the centre. You enter through peaceful Gothic cloisters with orange and lemon trees and a well at the centre. Inside the church is the tomb of Ramón Llull (1235–1316), the Catalan mystic who became a hermit following a failed seduction attempt and was later stoned to death attempting to convert Muslims in Tunisia. His statue can be seen on the Palma seafront; outside the basilica is a statue of another famous Mallorcan missionary, Fray Junípero Serra, who once lived in the monastery here. The streets behind the church, once home to jewellers and Jewish traders, are now rundown and seedy and best avoided after dark.

CASTELL DE BELLVER
(▶ 20, TOP TEN)

An impressive baroque portal gives relief to the stern façade of Palma's mighty Basílica de Sant Francesc

FUNDACIÓ JOAN MARCH
(MUSEU D'ART ESPANYOL CONTEMPORANI) ✪✪

The private collection of Mallorcan banker Joan March has been expanded into this small museum of 20th-century Spanish art, housed in an 18th-century mansion with Modernist touches. Among the artists featured are Picasso, Mir and Dalí, as well as Mallorcan avant-garde painter Michel Barcel.

- 35C3
- Carrer Sant Miquel 11
- 971 713515
- Mon–Fri 10–6:30, Sat 10–1:30
- Cafés in Plaça Major (£)
- None 👋 Cheap

FUNDACIÓ LA CAIXA ✪✪✪

The Gran Hotel was Palma's first luxury hotel when it opened in 1903. Designed by the Catalan architect Lluís Domènech i Montaner, it began the craze for *modernista* (art nouveau) architecture in the city. Restored by the Fundació la Caixa and reopened in 1993, it is now an art gallery with changing exhibitions and paintings by Hermen Anglada-Camarasa, founder of the 'Pollença school'. On the ground floor there is a bookshop and a trendy café-bar.

- 35C3
- Plaça Weyler 3
- 971 720111
- Tue–Sat 10–9, Sun 10–2
- Café and restaurant (££)
- Good
- 👋 Free

LA LLOTJA ✪✪

With twin turrets and an angel over the door, this 15th-century seafront building looks half-castle, half-church. In fact it is neither. It was designed by Guillem Sagrera (the architect of the cathedral's Portal del Mirador) as the city's exchange. Stand among the spiralling pillars, gaze up at the rib vaulting, and try to imagine the merchants of 500 years ago haggling over silk, spices and silver. Nowadays La Llotja is a cultural centre, hosting temporary exhibitions.

- 34A2
- Plaça Llotja
- 971 711705
- Tue–Sat 11–2, 5–9, Sun 11–2
- Wide choice of restaurants and bars near by (£–££)
- Good
- 👋 Free

Modern art, inside and out, at Fundació la Caixa – the 'in' place to meet for coffee and cakes

33

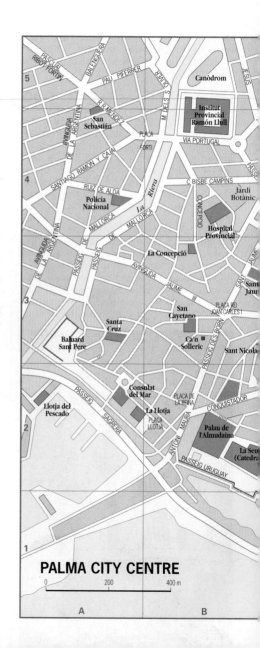

PALMA CITY CENTRE

0   200   400 m

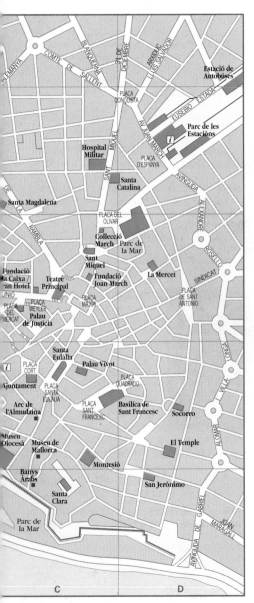

A statue of a Roman emperor stands at the foot of La Rambla

A Walk Around Palma

Distance
3.5km

Time
2 hours plus coffees,
browsing and visits – probably
half a day

Start/end point
Plaça d'Espanya

✚ 35D4

🚌 Most city buses
terminate here; island
buses terminate at the
nearby bus station on
Carrer Eusebi Estada

🚆 Trains from Inca and
Sóller also terminate here

Lunch
Fundació la Caixa (££)
✉ Plaça Weyler 3
☎ 971 728077

*Plaça Major – a good
place to stop for a coffee.
There is a craft market
held here on summer
mornings*

This walk starts in Plaça d'Espanya and passes close to all
of Palma's main sights. Begin by heading for Mercat Olivar
(▶ 37), where you can look round the market.

*Leave via Plaça Olivar and turn left into
Carrer Sant Miquel.*

Soon you reach Plaça Major with its outdoor cafés and
street entertainers.

*Continue across the square; fork right into
Carrer Jaume II.*

At the end of this pedestrian shopping street, don't fail to
look up at the *modernista* façade of Sa Nostra bank before
turning left into Plaça Cort. Beyond a gnarled olive tree you
see the town hall.

*Take the short street to the left of the town hall
to reach Plaça Santa Eulàlia; cross this square
diagonally and take Carrer Morey.*

This brings you into the heart of the
old city. Take your time here
admiring the courtyards; don't miss
Casa Oleza at No. 9.

*Continue straight on to Carrer
Miramar and turn right onto
the city walls.*

The cathedral (▶ 24–25) is above
you; to visit it and the palace, climb
the steps to a large wooden cross.

*Back on the walls, continue until you drop to the
S'Hort del Rei gardens (▶ 38). Cross Plaça
Reina and walk up the Born (▶ 39), turning
right by Bar Bosch into Carrer Unió.*

Look out for the old Gran Hotel (▶ 33) on your left and the
bakery opposite, two good examples of *modernista* style.
Beyond the theatre, the road bends left and becomes La
Rambla; stroll up this promenade among the flower stalls.

*At the top of La Rambla, turn right into Carrer
Oms and follow it back to Plaça d'Espanya.*

Fresh vegetables on sale in Mercat Olivar

MERCAT OLIVAR ✪✪
When you're tired of tourist sights and want to meet the people of Palma instead, head for this covered market. It is a feast for the eyes – huge piles of oranges, buckets full of olives, slabs of salt cod, fish you never knew existed. Those of a squeamish disposition should avoid the upstairs meat counters, where the pigs and rabbits look like pigs and rabbits rather than sterile pieces of packaged flesh. The market is a good place to buy ham and cheese, or you can stop for *tortilla* at one of the *tapas* stalls, where the workers drink brandy with their breakfast coffee.

- ✚ 35D4
- ✉ Plaça Olivar
- ☎ 971 720315
- 🕐 Mon–Sat 8–2
- 🍴 Several *tapas* bars (£) upstairs
- ✋ Free

MUSEU DIOCESÀ ✪
This small museum of religious and historical artefacts is based in a wing of the former episcopal palace tucked behind the cathedral. Among the paintings, pulpits and prayer books are splendid Arab tapestries, a collection of ceramics spanning five centuries and a 17th-century painting of baby Jesus carrying a cross. Look out for the portrait of St George (Sant Jordi) with medieval Palma in the background.

- ✚ 35C2
- ✉ Carrer Mirador 5
- ☎ 971 712827
- 🕐 Mon–Fri 10–1, 3–6, Sat–Sun 10–1:30
- ✋ Cheap
- ↪ La Seu (► 24–25)

MUSEU DE MALLORCA ✪✪
Mallorca's most important museum is housed in a 17th-century palace, with collections spanning more than 3,000 years of history. Start in the basement with the prehistory section, which includes pottery, metal and stone artefacts from the Talaiotic cultures, as well as bronze figures of naked warriors brought back from the Punic wars. Other rooms are devoted to Islamic archaeology, Gothic art (with a particularly fine collection of painted altarpieces), Modernism and 20th-century art.

- ✚ 35C2
- ✉ Carrer Portella 5
- ☎ 971 717540
- 🕐 Summer, Tue–Sat 10–2, 5–8, Sun 10–2; winter, Tue–Sat 10–1, 4–6, Sun 10–1
- 🍴 Bar Sa Murada (£) at foot of Carrer Portella
- ✋ Cheap

Palma's royal palace was built as a Muslim fortress and still has a very Islamic feel to it

➕ 34B2
✉ Carrer Palau Reial
☎ 971 727145
🕐 Palace: Apr–Sep, Mon–Fri 10–6:30, Sat 10–2; Oct–Mar, Mon–Fri 10–2, 4–6, Sat 10–2; Gardens: open access
♿ Wheelchair access on request
💷 Palace: moderate; Gardens: free
↔ La Seu (➤ 24–25)
❓ Still used by King Juan Carlos for official functions in Palma

PALAU DE L'ALMUDAINA ✪✪

A royal palace has stood on this site since the Muslim *walis* (governors) built their *alcázar* soon after the Arab conquest. It was converted into Gothic style under Jaume II, but elements of Islamic architecture remain – like the Moorish arches seen from the seafront, lit up at night like a row of lanterns. The courtyard, laid out in 1309 and flanked by palm trees, is at its best in late afternoon when the sun falls on the cathedral towers overhead. Just off the courtyard is the royal chapel, Capella de Santa Ana.

The S'Hort del Rei gardens beneath the palace make a pleasant place to sit beneath the fountains watching the world go by. Look out for the Arc de la Drassana, once the gateway to the royal docks; near here is a statue of a *hondero* or Balearic slinger. The gardens were rebuilt in the 1960s, forcing the demolition of several houses; their best-known landmark is Joan Miró's *Egg* sculpture, which few people can resist sticking their heads through.

➕ 35C1
🍴 Choice of cafés (£)
💷 Free
❓ Free concerts on summer evenings

PARC DE LA MAR ✪✪

Until the 1960s the sea reached up to the city walls, providing the perfect reflection for the cathedral. When the building of a new road changed all that, an artificial lake was constructed to reproduce the effect. The park around the lake is now a popular weekend and summer spot, with several cafés, outdoor concerts, a mural donated by Joan Miró and an art gallery in the vaults of the old city walls. Sit beneath the palm trees gazing up at the cathedral and try to imagine the travellers of days gone by arriving at this same spot from the sea by boat.

PASSEIG DES BORN ✪✪

For more than a century this short, tree-lined promenade has been at the heart of city life; it has witnessed *festas*, demonstrations and countless generations of families enjoying an evening stroll. During the Franco era it was renamed after the dictator, but everyone still called it 'the Born'. Come here to take the pulse of Palma from a seat at a pavement café – Bar Bosch, near the top of the Born in Plaça Rei Joan Carles I, is the traditional place. Near here is **Ca'n Solleric**, a modern art gallery which opened in 1995 in a converted mansion.

➕ 34B3
🍴 Wide choice of restaurants and cafés near by (£–££)

Ca'n Solleric
✉ Passeig des Born 27
☎ 971 722092
🕐 Tue–Sat 10–1:45, 5–8:30, Sun 10–1:45
🎟 Free

POBLE ESPANYOL (SPANISH VILLAGE) ✪

Spain gets the theme-park treatment at this 'village' in the outskirts of Palma, where reproductions of famous buildings from Córdoba, Toledo and Madrid are gathered together with typical houses from the Spanish regions. You can eat Spanish food in the Plaza Mayor (Spanish spellings here) or sit outside a café watching the tourists buy pearls and souvenirs at the village shops. A visit here gives you a whistle-stop tour of Spanish architecture, showing its development through Muslim and then Christian influences. If you have never been to Granada, it's worth coming just for the reproduction of the salon, baths and patio from the Alhambra Palace. Various artists give displays of handicrafts in workshops scattered throughout the 'village'.

➕ 72B2
✉ Carrer Poble Espanyol
☎ 971 737075
🕐 Apr–Nov, daily 9–8; Dec–Mar, daily 9–6:30
🍴 Restaurant and cafés (££)
🚌 5
🎟 Moderate
❓ Craft displays from 10 to one hour before closing time

'The Born' once hosted jousting contests but now the biggest battle is for a seat at a pavement café

LA SEU (► 24–25, TOP TEN)

A Walk by the Sea

Distance
3km one way

Time
1½ hours

Start point
Passeig Sagrera
 34A2
 1, 4, 15, 21

End point
Club de Mar
 1

Lunch
Taberna de la Boveda (££)
✉ Passeig Sagrera 3
☎ 971 720026

This walk along Palma's waterfront is good in the early morning, as the city stirs itself and the fish market comes to life; or late in the day as the sun sets over the sea, the pavement bars begin to buzz and the cathedral and castle light up for the night.

Start in Passeig Sagrera, at the foot of Avinguda d'Antoni Maura by the statue of Ramón Llull.

This short tree-lined avenue, named after the architect of La Llotja, passes several interesting buildings. First, La Llotja itself (▶ 33), Palma's masterpiece of Gothic civic architecture; Porta Vella del Moll, the old gateway to the city from the sea; and finally Consulat del Mar, the former maritime court which houses the Balearic government.

At the end of Passeig Sagrera, cross the main road to reach the fishing port, marked by lines of blue nets.

West of here, in a small garden, is the oratory of Sant Elm, designed as a navigators' chapel, later used as a tavern, and moved here stone by stone from Passeig Sagrera in 1947.

From here the walk is straightforward – just follow the seafront west along Passeig Marítim, using the promenade between the road and the sea. A cycle path, also used by joggers, runs alongside the promenade.

Pass Reial Club Nautic, facing a section of city wall and a row of windmills; look up ahead to see Bellver Castle on its hill. As you walk on, turn around to look back at the cathedral, seen across the bay through a forest of masts. From a jetty opposite the Auditorium theatre, excursion boats offer tours of Palma Bay. Keep going, and eventually you reach Club de Mar with its luxury yachts. Just beyond here is the commercial ferry port, where boats leave for Barcelona, Valencia, Menorca and Ibiza.

Return the same way, or take bus 1 back to Passeig Sagrera.

Around the Island

Each region of Mallorca has its own particular appeal – the northeast for history, the east coast for beaches and caves, the north and west for spectacular mountains and picture-postcard villages. And you haven't seen Mallorca until you have driven across *es pla*, the fertile plain at the centre of the island, with its almond groves, windmills and old market towns.

Try to do a bit of everything – one monastery, one mountain walk, one quiet cove – but don't try to do too much. The twisting mountain roads get very crowded in summer and journeys take longer than you think. Take your time and avoid the worst of the heat by doing what the Mallorcans do, break for a siesta. It is generally far more rewarding to spend a day pottering around one small area than to hare from one town to another ticking off the sights.

' If you would experience the most perfect method of travelling, ride upon a mule, under a Mediterranean sun, along a golden road that leads down from the mountains to the sea. '

GORDON WEST
Jogging Round Majorca (1929)

What to See Around the Island

ALCÚDIA (▶ 16, TOP TEN)

ALGAIDA ✪
Algaida is a typical Mallorcan town, all green shutters, narrow streets, a square lined with cafés and a huge sandstone church. Few visitors make it into the town centre; the attractions are all on the outskirts, on the Palma–Manacor road. The main one is **Ca'n Gordiola**, a glass factory housed in a mock castle. The ground floor contains a workshop (though it looks more like a church with its arches and stained glass) where you can watch glass being blown; upstairs there are museums devoted to both glass and perfume. A further 2km along the road to Manacor is a string of well-known restaurants, where the people of Palma head at weekends for old-fashioned Mallorcan cuisine.

ANDRATX ✪
Like many towns around the coast, Andratx was built several kilometres inland from its port in a bid to deter pirate raids. These days the town is reaping an unexpected benefit – tourists pour into the port, spending money which the town collects in taxes, yet except on market day Andratx sees little of the visitors and its people are left to get on with their lives. Surrounded by orange groves, and almond trees which leave a 'snowfall' of blossom each February, Andratx is a sleepy town which only really gets animated on Wednesdays when the streets are taken over by market stalls selling vegetables, cheeses and fish. When you have finished your shopping, climb to the top of the town to see the 13th-century church of Santa Maria.

✚ 28C3
🍴 Restaurants on the Palma–Manacor road (££)
🚌 From Palma
🔄 Puig de Randa (▶ 75)
❓ Market held Fri

Ca'n Gordiola
✉ Carretera Palma–Manacor, km19
☎ 971 665046
🕐 Apr–Oct, Mon–Sat 9–8, Sun 9–1; Nov–Mar, Mon–Sat 9–1:30, 3–7, Sun 9–1
🎫 Free

✚ 28A3
🍴 Bars and cafés (£)
🚌 Regular buses from Palma, Peguera and Port d'Andratx
🔄 Port d'Andratx (▶ 67), Sant Elm (▶ 79)
❓ Market held Wed

Almonds from the orchards around Andratx are one of the bargains you can pick up in the weekly market

The West

Distance
62km

Time
3 hours plus lunch and time at
La Granja

Start/end point
Andratx
✚ 28A3

Lunch
La Granja (£)
☎ 971 610032

*You pass several coastal
watchtowers, including
this one near the village
of Estellencs*

This drive gives an excellent introduction to the mountain
and coastal scenery of western Mallorca.

> *Start in Andratx, taking the C710 to Estellencs
> about halfway up the main street.*

Immediately the road begins to climb through pine woods
and tunnels, with occasional glimpses of the sea. Follow
this beautiful twisting coast road to the village of
Estellencs, one of the prettiest in Mallorca, with narrow,
steep cobbled streets and women doing their washing at
the village well. After another 5km, stop at the Mirador de
Ses Animes and clamber up to the 16th-century watchtower for views right along the northwest coast. Soon
after this you reach Banyalbufar (▶ 46), with its
spectacular terracing.

> *When the C710 turns off left towards
> Valldemossa, keep straight on the PM110,
> signposted to Palma. After 1km you see a sign to
> La Granja on your right.*

You could easily spend 2–3
hours at this display of Mallorcan
traditions (▶ 57).

> *Leaving La Granja, take
> the narrow road to
> Puigpunyent from the
> car park.*

Follow this road for 10km, a
dramatic journey through olive
groves in the shadow of Puig de
Galatzó. The road continues
through Puigpunyent and on to
Galilea (▶ 56), a mountain village
with a couple of *tapas* bars and
views out to sea. From here the
road twists and turns down to
the village of Es Capdella.

> *Turn right in the village
> and follow signs back to
> Andratx.*

A flight of steps leads to Artà's hilltop sanctuary

ARTÀ ✪✪

Derived from the Arabic word *jertan* ('garden'), Artà has been occupied for at least 3,000 years, as evidenced by the remains of a Bronze Age site at Ses Païsses (► 85) just outside the town. Nowadays Artà is a prosperous little town near the coast, which gets particularly lively each Tuesday on market day.

From the parish church of Transfiguració del Senyor, an avenue of cypress trees leads to Artà's crowning glory, its hilltop fortress and Santuari de Sant Salvador. The view down over the rooftops, a jumble of tiles in every shade of brown, is one of the sights of Mallorca. On the site of a Moorish fortress, the original sanctuary walls and chapel were rebuilt in the 19th century. Walk around the battlements, rest in a peaceful courtyard, then look into the sanctuary church with its vivid paintings of two Mallorcan heroes – Jaume the Conqueror receiving the surrender of the *walis*, and Ramón Llull being stoned to death in Tunisia. There is also a painting of Sant Antoni, patron saint of Artà, and of animals, seen here, as always, with a small pig. Each January the saint is commemorated with a masked procession and a blessing of pets. Artà's big festival, Sant Antoni de Juny, dates back to 1581 and features dancers with cardboard horses strapped to their hips.

Artà's small **museum**, housed inside Sa Nostra bank, has archaeological discoveries from Greek and Roman periods.

✚ 29E4
🍴 Several bars and restaurants (£–££)
🚌 From Palma and Cala Rajada
🔁 Ses Païsses (► 85)
❓ Market held Tue; Sant Antoni Abat, procession and blessing of pets, 16–17 Jan; Sant Antoni de Juny, *cavallets* horse dances, 13 Jun

Museum
✉ Carrer Estrella 4
☎ 971 835017
🕐 Mon–Fri 10–1
 Cheap

AUTO-SAFARI (SAFARI-ZOO) ✪

Mallorca's only zoo consists of a 4-km drive through open countryside, passing giraffes, zebra, flamingos and deer (keep your car windows shut against marauding monkeys), followed by a 'baby zoo' with elephants, crocodiles and various young animals. You can also explore the 44-hectare reserve by a special 'mini-train' for which you pay a hefty supplement on top of the already considerable cost of entry.

✚ 29F3
✉ Carretera Porto Cristo–Son Servera, km5
☎ 971 810909
🕐 Apr–Sep, daily 9–7; Oct–Mar, daily 9–5
🍴 Café (£)
♿ Good
💶 Expensive

BANYALBUFAR ✪✪

People come to Banyalbufar to see one thing – its terraced hillsides, sloping down to the sea. Developed by the Moors and divided by drystone walls, these terraces speak powerfully of man's ingenuity in creating farmland out of inhospitable cliffs. Until recently it was the custom for each generation to add a further tier. In Moorish times the town, whose Arabic name means 'vineyard by the sea', was famed for its Malvasia wine – nowadays the terraces are mostly used to grow vegetables, though a few vines have been planted once again. Banyalbufar's popularity with foreign artists has led some people to conclude that it will be the next Deià (▶ 22).

✚ 28B4
🍴 Café Bellavista (£)
🚌 Bus from Palma
↔ La Granja (▶ 57)

The terraced slopes of Banyalbufar, created over a thousand years, reach right down to the sea

BINISSALEM ✪

If you order Mallorcan wine in a restaurant, it will probably come from Binissalem. Viticulture was introduced here by the Romans and has survived in much reduced form. The reputation of Binissalem red wines, made with the local grape Manto Negro, has been growing in recent years – the best-known *bodega*, José L Ferrer, is on the right as you enter the town from Palma. Binissalem is a handsome town with a well-preserved old quarter; a Sunday-morning craft market is held in the main square.

✚ 28C4
🍴 Several restaurants and bars (££)
🚆 Train from Palma and Inca
↔ Inca (▶ 58)
❓ Market held Fri, Sun; wine festival last weekend in Sep

CABRERA

'Goat island' is the largest in a rocky archipelago lying 20km off the south coast. Pliny claimed it as the birthplace of Hannibal; during the Napoleonic Wars it became a notorious prison camp. Since 1991 the island has been a protected national park. You can only get there on a day trip by boat, with time to walk up to the 14th-century castle above the harbour, visit a museum housed in an old wine cellar and swim in the Blue Grotto on the way back.

✚ 29D1
⛴ From Colònia de Sant Jordi, May–Oct, daily 9:30 (☎ 971 649034)
↔ Colònia de Sant Jordi (▶ 51)

CALA DE SANT VICENÇ ✪✪

This old-fashioned holiday resort has recently been given a facelift and is in danger of becoming chic. It is still very popular with Mallorcans, especially on summer weekends. Four small coves, each with their own beach, huddle together beneath Cavall Bernat, a limestone ridge which casts its shadow into the sea. A walk of around 45 minutes leads across the hills to Port de Pollença (➤ 70).

🕂 29D5
🍴 Bars and restaurants (£–£££)
🚌 Bus from Pollença

CALA D'OR ✪✪

Each of the various *calas* (bays) along the east coast has its own distinctive character; in the case of Cala d'Or the word is 'chic'. Former fishing harbours have been turned into marinas; people come here to sail and dive, and drink champagne at waterfront bars. The villas are white and flat-roofed, in Ibizan style, designed in the 1930s by Pep Costa Ferrer, and the effect is surprisingly attractive. Nowadays Cala d'Or is the collective name for a string of resorts, beaches and coves; they include Porto Petro, around a horseshoe bay 2km to the south, and Cala Mondragó, a further 4km south, where a pair of sandy beaches form part of the Mondragó nature reserve.

🕂 29E2
🍴 Wide choice of restaurants (££–£££)
🚌 From Palma

CALA FIGUERA ✪✪

More than anywhere else in Mallorca, Cala Figuera retains the atmosphere of a working fishing port. White-painted houses reach down to the water's edge and fishermen sit on the steps mending nets. If you get here early enough in the morning you might even see the catch coming in. A path follows around the tiny harbour and onto the cliffs, offering good views back towards the bay. The nearest beach is 4km to the south at Cala Santanyí.

🕂 29E2
🍴 Several seafood restaurants and others (££)
🚌 From Palma and Santanyí
🔁 Santanyí (➤ 82)

Fishermen's cottages at Cala Figuera

CALA MILLOR ✪

Fifty years ago this was a lonely dune-covered shore; now it has become the major resort on Mallorca's east coast. The main attraction is its fine sandy beaches; from Cala Bona ('the good bay') to Cala Millor ('the better bay') they stretch unbroken for 2km. In summer it is 'lively', travel-agent speak for brash, and best avoided unless you like discos and late-night bars; in winter it takes on a new atmosphere, as a resort for the 'young at heart', another travel-agent euphemism. To see what this coast used to be like, walk to the headland at Punta de n'Amer (➤ 76).

✚ 29F3
🍴 Wide choice of bars and restaurants (£–££)
🚌 From Palma; also from Cala Rajada and Port d'Alcúdia in summer
↔ Punta de n'Amer (➤ 76)

Cala Millor – the golden sands just go on and on

CALA RAJADA ✪

This fishing port on Mallorca's eastern tip, surrounded by fine beaches and pretty coves, has become a popular summer resort, with windsurfing, snorkelling and numerous discos. Many Germans have second homes here; there have been complaints in the Mallorcan press that it is becoming a 'German colony'.

A short walk uphill from the beach leads through woodland to the lighthouse at Punta de Capdepera. Also above the harbour are the Jardins Casa March, owned by the same banking family as the Fundació Joan March in Palma. The gardens contain a sculpture park with works by Rodin, Henry Moore and modern Catalan artists. They can only be visited by prior arrangement with the tourist office.

The other reason for coming here is to make a day trip to Menorca (➤ 121). Fast boats leave each morning for the Menorcan city of Ciutadella, with its Gothic cathedral and harbourside fish restaurants.

✚ 29F4
🍴 Wide choice of restaurants (££)
🚌 From Palma and Porto Cristo; also from Cala Millor in summer
🚢 Day trips to Menorca (☎ 902 100444)
ℹ Tourist office: Plaça dels Pins (☎ 971 563033)
↔ Capdepera (➤ 50)
❓ Market held Sat; processions of boats, 16 July; summer festival of evening concerts in Jardins Casa March

CALVIÀ ✪

Calvià is like an old lady who has won the *lotería* and doesn't know how to cope with her success. Until recently an unassuming country town, Calvià hit the jackpot when tourists discovered the nearby beaches and it is now said to be the richest municipality in Spain. There are a few

✚ 28B3
🍴 Choice of restaurants and bars (££)
🚌 20 from Palma
❓ Market held Mon

Tales of old Calvià in this ceramic display, created by local arts students to introduce visitors to the history of their town

ostentatious signs of wealth, like the sparkling new town hall and sports stadium, but mostly life continues as before, with ochre-coloured houses, a handful of shops and bars, and chickens scrambling between the olive trees. The town is dominated by the church of Sant Joan Baptista, built in the late 19th century around the 13th-century original; near here, by a fountain, a ceramic mural tells the story of Calvià's history. Founded in 1249 with 80 inhabitants, the town had a population of 3,000 in 1960 and 11,560 in 1980 – all because of tourism. Stand on the terrace looking out over almond and carob trees and it is hard to believe you are just a few kilometres from the teeming resorts of 'Maganova'.

CAMPOS ✪

Midway from Llucmajor to Santanyí on the C717, Campos was founded by Jaume II in 1300 on the site of earlier Roman and Arab settlements. A painting of Christ by the Sevillian artist Murillo hangs in the parish church of Sant Julià. Next door to the church is a museum with a large collection of offertory bowls. To visit both the church and the museum, meet the parish priest outside the church door at 11AM for a guided tour. Campos has a busy market on Thursdays and Saturdays and its port adjoins the resort of Colònia de Sant Jordi (► 51) to the south.

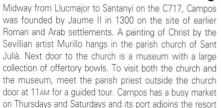

🚩 29D2
🍴 Several cafés and bars (£)
🚌 From Palma
❓ Market held Thu, Sat

Església de Sant Julià
✉ Carrer Bisbe Talladas 17
☎ 971 650003
🕐 Mon–Sat 11AM
💰 Donation requested

CAP DE FORMENTOR (▶ 18, TOP TEN)

CAPDEPERA   ✪✪

➕ 29F4

🍴 Café de l'Orient, Plaça de l'Orient (£)

🚌 From Palma and Cala Rajada

🔁 Cala Rajada (▶ 48)

❓ Market held Wed; Nostra Senyora de la Esperança *festa*, 18 Dec

Castle

☎ 971 818746

🕐 Apr–Oct, daily 10–8; Nov–Mar, daily 10–5

💶 Cheap

If you are driving between Artà and Cala Rajada, stop off to visit this small town, crowned by the largest fortress in Mallorca. The Romans were the first to build a **castle** on this site – the Moors enlarged it, the Christians destroyed it, then replaced it with one of their own in the 14th century. Legend has it that the citizens of Capdepera hid in the castle when under siege, placing an image of Our Lady of Hope on the battlements, and the invaders were driven away by fog. The miracle is recorded inside the castle in the Capella de Nostra Senyora de la Esperança and remembered each year at the town's annual *festa*. You reach the castle by climbing the steps from the market square, Plaça de l'Orient.

CAPOCORB VELL   ✪✪

➕ 28C2

✉ Carretera Cap Blanc–Llucmajor

☎ 971 180155

🕐 Fri–Wed 10–5

🍴 Near by (£)

💶 Cheap

These are the most significant remains of the Talaiotic culture, which flourished in Mallorca between around 1300 and 800 BC. Villages were dominated by *talaiots*, circular or rectangular structures two to three storeys high, which were used as both burial chambers and defensive forts. Each settlement was surrounded by Cyclopean walls, built from massive, unhewn stones without mortar to hold them together. There is no evidence of a written language, so the stones are all that archaeologists have to go on in understanding prehistoric Mallorcan culture. At Capocorb Vell, 12km south of Llucmajor, you can see five *talaiots* and wander around the ancient village, 100m above sea level just inland from the coast. The Talaiotic people kept sheep, and the sound of sheep bells in the nearby fields is a touching reminder of continuity.

Capdepera's castle dominates the views of the town as you approach

CASTELL D'ALARÓ (► 19, TOP TEN)

COLÒNIA DE SANT JORDI ✪

Once the port for the market town of Campos, Colònia de Sant Jordi is now a busy resort, on a rocky promontory close to Mallorca's southern tip. Its small beach looks out over several islets, with good views all the way to Cabrera (► 46). There are two further sandy beaches to the east, and the long stretch of Platja Es Trenc begins just west of town. To the north are the hot springs of Banys de Sant Joan. The main reason for coming here, though, is to take the boat trip to Cabrera.

COSTA NORD ✪✪

The American actor Michael Douglas could be seen as a 21st-century successor to Archduke Ludwig Salvator (► 88, 89), using his money and his influence to promote the landscapes and culture of Mallorca. In 2000 he opened Costa Nord, a multimedia cultural centre in Valldemossa devoted to Mallorca's north coast. The visit begins with a short film, narrated by Douglas, in which he describes his love for the island; it continues with a recreation of the Archduke's yacht, the *Nixe*, accompanied by a commentary on his Mediterranean voyages. The shop sells a range of pricey souvenirs; there is also a café, a restaurant and a concert hall which attracts top international names during the Mediterranean Nights festival each summer. Costa Nord is a personal tribute to an island which, as Douglas says, has attracted 'poets, painters… and yes, film stars'.

🚩 29D2
🍴 Choice of restaurants
🚌 From Palma
🔄 Cabrera (► 46), Ses Salines (► 85)
❓ Market held Wed

🚩 28B4
✉ Avinguda Palma 6, Valldemossa
☎ 971 616070
🕐 Summer, Tue–Sun 10–8; winter, Tue–Sun 10–6
🍴 Bar and restaurant (££)
🚌 From Palma and Deià
💰 Expensive
🔄 Valldemossa (► 26)
❓ Mediterranean Nights, Jun–Aug

Watersports and sandy beaches at Colònia de Sant Jordi

In the Know

If you only have a short time to visit Mallorca, or would like to get a real flavour of the island, here are some ideas:

10
Ways To Be A Local

Try to learn a little of the language, Catalan as well as Spanish – a simple *bon dia* goes a long way.
Relax, take your time and settle into the Mediterranean way of life.
Take a siesta to avoid the afternoon sun – have a long lunch, or rest in the shade.
Do everything late – a late lunch, a late supper, a very late night.
Join the evening *passeig* to see and be seen – put on your best clothes and pop into a bar for *tapas* and a chilled sherry.
Change out of your beachwear for restaurants, shops and churches – Mallorcans rarely dress formally but they always manage to look smart.
Find a local *festa* and get swept along with the crowd.

Go walking in the mountains at weekends, or join a *romeria* (pilgrimage) to a hilltop church.
Respect the local environment – don't drop litter or pick wild flowers.
Drink your coffee strong and sweet, with a touch of brandy, whatever the time of day.

10
Good Places To Have Lunch

Bon Lloc (£) ✉ Carrer Sant Feliu 7, Palma ☎ 971 718617. You won't find better value than this four-course vegetarian lunch. 🕐 Closed Sun.
Caballito de Mar (££–£££) ✉ Passeig Sagrera 5, Palma ☎ 971 721074. Fish restaurant perfectly placed to catch the winter sun. 🕐 Closed Mon.
Ca N'Antuna (££) ✉ Carrer Arbona Colom 8,

Fornalutx ☎ 971 633068. Dine on a terrace overlooking the orange groves. 🕐 Closed Mon.
Celler Sa Font (££) ✉ Plaça d'Espanya 18, Sineu ☎ 971 520313. Where the farmers go after Sineu's Wed market.
Centro (£) ✉ Avinguda Bisbe Campins 13, Porreres ☎ 971 168372. Huge portions, excellent food, ridiculous prices – in a church hall. 🕐 Closed Sun.
Es Verger (££) ✉ On the way to Castell d'Alaró ☎ 971 182126. Farmhouse restaurant specialising in roast lamb from a wood-burning oven.
La Gran Tortuga (££) ✉ Aldea Cala Fornells 1, Peguera ☎ 971 686023. Eat and swim on a terrace overlooking the sea. 🕐 Closed Mon.
Puig de Sant Miquel (££) ✉ Carretera de Manacor, km 31 ☎ 971 646314. Roast kid and other Mallorcan specialities beside a hilltop sanctuary near Montuïri.
Stay (£££) ✉ Moll Nou, Port de Pollença ☎ 971 864013. Fresh

Port de Sóller, seen from the Mirador de Ses Barques

fish beside the harbour.
Taberna de la Boveda
(££) ✉ Passeig Sagrera 3,
Palma ☎ 971 720026.
Great *tapas* on the water-
front. 🕐 Closed Sun.

10
Top Activities

Birdwatching: the best
areas are the S'Albufera
wetlands, the salt flats
around Ses Salines, and
Gorg Blau and Cúber
reservoirs between Sóller
and Lluc.
Cricket: have a game with
the MCC – Magaluf Cricket
Club ☎ 971 233262.
Cycling: bike hire is
available in resorts and at
Ciclos Bimont ✉ Plaça
Progrés 19, Palma
☎ 971 731866.
Fishing: you need a
licence – enquire at tourist
offices.
Golf: there are 15 courses
(▶ 113).

Horse riding: several
centres have classes for all
abilities. Contact Federació
Balear Hípica ✉ Avinguda
Joan Miró 17, Palma
☎ 971 456729.
Sailing: more than 40
marinas. The national
sailing school is at
Avinguda Joan Miró, Cala
Major ☎ 971 402512.
Scuba diving: clubs in
Palma, Port d'Andratx and
Santa Ponça (▶ 114).
Walking: especially in the
Serra de Tramuntana. Take
a map, compass, sun hat
and plenty of water.
Windsurfing: equipment
can be hired at most of the
main resorts.

5
Good Beaches

- Cala Millor
- Es Trenc (nudist)
- Formentor
- Magaluf
- Platja de Palma

10
Best Viewpoints

- Castell d'Alaró
- Castell de Bellver
- Ermita de Bonany
- Mirador de Ses Animes,
  Banyalbufar
- Mirador de Ses Barques,
  Sóller–Lluc road
- Parc de la Mar, Palma
- Puig de Randa
- Puig de Santa Eugènia
- Puig de Teix, near Deià
- Santuari de Sant
  Salvador

5
Quiet Coves

- Cala de Deià
- Cala Mesquida (north of
  Capdepera)
- Cala Pi
- Cala Tuent (near Sa
  Calobra)
- Portals Vells

COVES D'ARTÀ (► 21, TOP TEN)

COVES DEL DRAC (DRAGON CAVES)

CUEVAS
DEL
DRACH

Dank, dark and humid, these limestone caves on the edge of Porto Cristo have become one of Mallorca's top tourist sights. Groups of several hundred people at a time are herded along 2km of slippery paths by guides who tell you in four languages how to interpret the bizarre stalactite formations – a cactus here, a flag there, the Fairies' Theatre, Diana's Bath... You might just think they resemble thousands of spiky parsnips hanging from the ceiling. Try to imagine how Walt Disney would conjure up a fabulous witches' cave and you have the idea. The one-hour tour ends with a floodlit, floating violin concert on Lake Martel, Europe's largest underground lake, named after the French geologist Édouard Martel who first explored these caves in the late 19th century at the commission of Archduke Ludwig Salvator. Afterwards you can return by boat across the lake to the exit.

COVES DELS HAMS

You cannot miss these caves as you drive from Manacor to Porto Cristo. Most people only want to visit one set of caves and the giant billboards and flags at the entrance are an attempt to ensure that this is the one. In fact you are better off continuing to the Coves del Drac (► above) or up the coast to the Coves d'Artà (► 21). But for serious speleologists, here are the facts. The caves were discovered by Pedro Caldentey in 1905 and the electric lighting was added by his son. Their name means 'fish-hooks', which the stalactites are said to resemble. You get a guided tour and, yes, another concert on an underground lake.

DEIÀ (► 22, TOP TEN)

29E3
971 820753
Apr–Oct, tours on the hour 10–5; Nov–Mar, tours at 10:45, 12, 2, 3:30
Café (£)
From Palma and Cala Rajada
None
Expensive
Porto Cristo (► 74), Coves dels Hams (► below), Acuàrium de Mallorca (► 109)

29E3
Carretera Manacor–Porto Cristo
971 820988
Apr–Oct, daily 10–6; Nov–Mar, daily 10:30–5:30
Café-restaurant (£)
None
Expensive
Porto Cristo (► 74), Coves del Drac (► above)

ERMITA DE BONANY

This hilltop hermitage is where Junípero Serra preached his last sermon in Mallorca before leaving to found the Mexican and Californian missions. The views from the terrace, covering almost the entire plain, are superb. You can stay here in simple cells, but unlike other monasteries it has no restaurant or bar – just a chapel and a small shop selling religious trinkets.

29D3
☎ 971 561101
🍴 Free
↔ Petra (▶ 64)

> ### Did you know ?
>
> Bon any *means good year.*
> *The first church was built here in 1604; five years later,
> during a drought, the villagers of Petra
> climbed to the chapel to pray for rain. When their
> prayers were answered with a* bon any, *they named
> their sanctuary Bonany.*

FELANITX

Felanitx is at the centre of Mallorca's second wine-producing area and it is also known for its capers, or 'green pearls'. You can buy them at the Sunday morning market, which spills out onto the streets around the church of Sant Miquel, with local pottery displayed on the church steps. The church façade contains a memorial to 414 people who died when a wall collapsed in 1844; further up, beneath the rose window, you can see the archangel Michael standing on the Devil's head.

29E3
🍴 Bars and cafés (£)
🚌 From Palma and Porto Colom
↔ Santuari de Sant Salvador (▶ 82)
❓ Market held Sun; Sant Agusti, *cavallets* horse dances, 28 Aug

FORNALUTX

Fornalutx, in the hills above Sóller, calls itself the prettiest village in Spain, and it is hard to disagree – unless you accept the claims of its neighbour Biniaraix. There are several terrace restaurants and bars, where you can sit and soak in the views of olive and orange groves climbing ever higher until they reach the pine-clad foothills of Puig Major.

28C4
🍴 Several restaurants (££)
↔ Sóller (▶ 86)

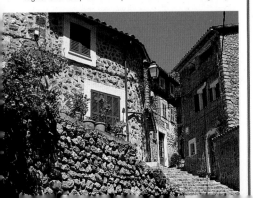

The prettiest village in Spain? Go and judge for yourself

⊞ 72B2
✉ Carrer Joan de Saridakis 29, Cala Major
☎ 971 701420
⏲ 15 May–15 Sep, Tue–Sat 10–7, Sun 10–3; 16 Sep–14 May, Tue–Sat 10–6, Sun 10–3
🍴 Café (£)
🚌 4 from Palma
♿ Good
ⓘ Moderate

FUNDACIÓ PILAR I JOAN MIRÓ ●●

The painter and sculptor Joan Miró spent most of his life in Barcelona, but both his wife and mother were Mallorcan and he always longed to return to the scene of his childhood holidays to draw inspiration from what he called 'the light of Mallorca'. In 1956, aged 63, he bought a house and studio in Cala Major. He lived here until he died in 1983 after which it was enlarged to hold a permanent exhibition of his works.

The collection includes more than 100 paintings, 25 sculptures and 3,000 studio pieces but only a small amount is displayed at any time. The paintings are almost childish, all vivid splashes of bright primary colours, influenced by his love of peasant traditions and his fascination with *siurells* (clay whistles). Anyone tempted to remark that their child could do better should take a look at the heavily realistic work that Miró was producing aged eight – the fantasy came later. Works on display include the draft for UNESCO's *Mural del Sol* in Paris.

Glance into Miró's studio, left untouched since his death, with work in progress, open tins of paint and black stains all over the floor.

The Wind amongst the Bulrushes by Joan Miró (1971)

⊞ 28B3
🍴 Two bars (£)
↔ La Reserva (► 76)

GALILEA ●●

This pretty village, 460m above sea level, in the shadow of the great peak of Puig de Galatzó, gets crowded out by day trippers who come to sample the views from the church terrace. On a good day you can see far out to sea, while eating *tapas* outside the church and listening to the echo of sheep-bells on the hillsides. The nearby village of Puigpunyent is also justifiably popular and is surrounded by orange groves – as well as being the base for visiting La Reserva (► 76).

LA GRANJA ✪✪

This country house, just south of Banyalbufar, is on a site known since Roman times for its natural spring. When Jaume I conquered Mallorca he divided the island into four feudal estates, giving one to Count Nuno Sanç, who settled at La Granja. In 1239 the Count handed the estate to Cistercian monks to found Mallorca's first monastery. Since 1447 it has been a private house owned by various noble families; most of what you see today dates from the 17th century.

Highlights of the tour include an aristocratic drawing-room with its own theatre, the family chapel and a dungeon with a torture chamber – but the real reason for visiting La Granja is to learn about rural Mallorcan traditions. Workshops, cellars and kitchens contain displays of everyday objects. And on Wednesday and Friday afternoons, women in traditional costume give demonstrations of lacemaking, embroidery and spinning, donkeys turn threshing-wheels and there are tastings of cheese, wine, sausages, doughnuts and fig cake. Look carefully and you just might see a tray of *coca* (Mallorcan pizza) being removed from the restaurant oven and carried to the medieval kitchens to be served beside a log fire. There are also displays of bagpipe music and folk dancing, which are entertaining if not terribly authentic.

Escape from the tour groups by walking in the grounds, which contain botanical gardens, waterfalls and a thousand-year-old yew – there is a 1,200-m signed walk. And look out for the exhibit listed in the guide as 'dog' – it is just that, a *ca de bestiar*, or black-coated Mallorcan guard dog on a chain.

If you have not gorged yourself on free samples, the restaurant serves good Mallorcan staples like *pa amb oli* and *sopes mallorquines*.

✚ 28B4
☎ 971 610032
🕐 Apr–Sep, daily 10–7;
   Oct–Mar, daily 10–6
🍴 Restaurant (£)
🚌 From Palma
♿ None
💰 Expensive
↔ Banyalbufar (➤ 46)
❓ Folk fiesta, Wed, Fri 3–5

The estate at La Granja has been turned into a living museum, where staff dressed in folk costume give displays of Mallorcan traditions

57

INCA ✪

Mallorca's third-largest town styles itself 'city of leather', and if you come on an organised tour you will undoubtedly be taken to a leather factory. Shop around; the bargains these days are few and far between. Better to come on Thursdays, when the streets around Plaça d'Espanya are taken over by Mallorca's largest weekly market. Plenty of leather here, of varying quality, plus jewellery, carved olive-wood, lace and fresh produce from across the island. Plaça d'Espanya itself becomes an open-air flower show. Near here are a smart coffee-house, Café Mercantil, with uphol-stered leather chairs, and Ca'n Delante (🔲 Carrer Major 27), one of Mallorca's top pastry shops. Inca is also known for its *cellers*, old wine-cellars turned into restaurants featuring traditional dishes at reasonable prices.

JARDINS DE ALFÁBIA ✪✪

These classical gardens by the entrance to the Sóller tunnel are a legacy of the Arab talent for landscaping and irrigation. Their name derives from *al fabi*, 'jar of olives' in Arabic. They were probably designed by Benihabet, the Muslim governor of Inca who converted to Christianity following the Spanish invasion.

A flight of steps lined with tall palms leads to a covered walkway – from here you can strike off to see lily ponds, bamboo groves or citrus trees growing in the shadow of the mountains. If you have just driven over the Coll de Sóller and are in need of a rest, this would make a lovely spot for a siesta. Take a book or some postcards, find a seat in the shade, then drift off to sleep to the sound of gently flowing water.

LLUC (► 23, TOP TEN)

LLUC-ALCARI ✪

You could easily miss Mallorca's smallest village, which consists of little more than a bend in the Deià–Sóller road. With just a handful of houses and a hotel, it would make an ideal base for a walking holiday in the nearby mountains. The views are postcard-perfect – in fact you are far more likely to see it on a postcard than you are to actually go there. Picasso once lived in the village during a short stay on Mallorca.

LLUCMAJOR

This ordinary country town, the largest in southern Mallorca, has a place in history – it was the site of the battle in 1349 where Pedro IV of Aragón killed his relative Jaume III to end Mallorca's brief spell as an independent kingdom. Jaume's death is commemorated by a statue at the end of Passeig Jaume III. Near by, on Carrer Obispo Taxaquet, is another statue in honour of Llucmajor's cobblers. Shoemaking is still a significant industry here. Almonds and apricots grow around the town and make good buys at the market, held twice a week in Plaça d'Espanya.

28C3
Cafés and bars (£)
From Palma
Puig de Randa (► 75)
Market held Wed, Sun

MAGALUF

More than anywhere else in Mallorca, Magaluf has been blighted by the curse of mass tourism. During the 1980s it became a byword for all that was wrong with Mallorca; foreign TV crews would flock here to film drinking competitions, wet T-shirt contests and teenagers throwing up on the beach. However, in the 1990s Magaluf tried hard to change its image. High-rise hotels have been destroyed, a new seafront promenade has been built, and the council has introduced activities from guided walks to *tai chi* on the beach. But still the lager louts come... and if you want cheap sun, sea, sand and *sangría*, there's no better place.

28B3
Huge choice of bars and restaurants (£)
Regular buses from Palma
Palma Nova (► 63), Portals Vells (► 72)

Magaluf – never mind the lager louts, the beach is superb

➕ 29E3

🍴 Several bars and cafés (£)

🚌 From Palma and Porto Cristo

❓ Market held Mon

Perlas Majórica

✉ Avinguda Majórica 48

☎ 971 550200

🕐 Mon–Fri 9–1, 2:30–7, Sat–Sun 10–1

🎫 Free

Setting pearls into their gold surrounds at a factory in Manacor

MANACOR ✪

Mallorca's second city is the nearest thing the island has to an industrial town. Despite the lack of obvious sights, the narrow streets behind the church make a pleasant place to stroll and soak up the atmosphere of everyday Mallorca. The church, Església dels Delors de Nostra Senyora, was built on the site of a mosque and its minaret-style tower can be seen for miles. Look inside to see the figure of Christ with scrawny hair and a skirt – pilgrims queue up to kiss his bloodstained feet.

Almost every visitor to Manacor ends up at a pearl factory – **Perlas Majórica** is the best-known. Mallorca's artificial pearl industry produces 50 million pearls a year, using the scales of a million fish, so do not imagine they are a safe alternative for your vegetarian friends. They are said to be indistinguishable from the real thing, and almost as expensive.

➕ 29D3

🍴 Restaurants and bars (£)

🚌 From Palma

🔄 Algaida (▶ 43), Vilafranca de Bonany (▶ 90)

❓ Market held Mon; Sant Bartomeu festival, 24 Aug; Fira de la Perdiu (partridge and hunting fair), first Sun in Dec

MONTUÏRI ✪

High on a ridge surrounded by old stone windmills, the village of Montuïri is probably the most impressive sight along the Palma–Manacor road. The eight mill-towers of the Molinar district, redundant since the 1920s, are the symbol of the village; the best views are from the Ermita de Sant Miquel, a 19th-century hermitage on top of a small hill 2km to the east. Montuïri is the setting for one of Mallorca's most spectacular festivals: each August *Cossiers*, accompanied by dancers with bagpipes, flutes and drums, dress up as women and devils and perform a dance, the origins of which stretch back at least 400 years, where evil is overcome by good.

The Northeast

This leisurely half-day drive takes in several family attractions close to the northeast coast. It can easily be done as a day trip from Palma, adding 1½ hours to the time.

Begin by the OlivArt factory shop, as you enter Manacor on the C715 from Palma. Follow signs to Porto Cristo, leaving Manacor along a boulevard with palm trees down the middle.

After 13km you see the Coves dels Hams (➤ 54) – choose between stopping here or continuing to Porto Cristo for the Coves del Drac (➤ 54).

Take the bypass around Porto Cristo, or drive down to the seafront, where you turn left up a steep hill, following signs to Cala Millor.

A word in your ear – you never know who you might meet on a drive around Safari-Zoo

The road leads through orchards divided by drystone walls, reaching Safari-Zoo (➤ 45), where you can drive around the zoo.

Continue north, bypassing Cala Millor and turning left into Son Servera. Turn right towards Capdepera (➤ 50).

Long before you get there you see the castle crowning the village on a hill. Stop here for lunch and a climb to the castle, then if you feel like an afternoon on the beach take the side road to Cala Mesquida.

Otherwise take the C715 to Artà.

After exploring Artà (➤ 45), take to the coast.

Follow the C712 coast road around the bay of Alcúdia, with the dark silhouette of Cap de Formentor looming up ahead of you.

You pass the S'Albufera nature reserve (➤ 77) before finally reaching Alcúdia (➤ 16).

Return to Palma in under an hour by taking the C713 and joining the motorway at Inca.

Distance
80km

Time
4 hours including visits to a cave and the zoo

Start point
Manacor
✚ 29E3

End point
Alcúdia
✚ 29D5

Lunch
Café l'Orient (£)
✉ Plaça de l'Orient, Capdepera
☎ 971 563098

✚ 29D4
❓ Sun market; Revelta de Sant Antoni, 16–17 Jan
🚆 Train from Palma

Museu Etnòlogic de Mallorca
✉ Carrer Major 15
☎ 971 717540
🕓 Apr–Sep, Tue–Sat 10–2, 5–8, Sun 10–1; Oct–Mar, Tue–Sat 10–1, 4–6, Sun 10–1
✋ Cheap

Revealing Mallorca's past

MURO   ✪✪

This small town between Inca and the S'Albufera marshes has one overriding attraction – the **Museu Etnòlogic de Mallorca**. This museum, housed in a former mansion, gives fascinating glimpses into Mallorca's past. The kitchen contains pottery similar to what you see in the markets today; the recreated pharmacy has a pair of scales in the shape of a crucifix. Upstairs there is a fine collection of *siurells* (clay whistles) featuring men on horseback, carrying water and playing guitars. A courtyard with a well, a waterwheel and orange trees leads to more exhibits – blacksmith's and cobbler's workshops, a collection of carriages, and tools once used by silversmiths, sculptors and spoonmakers.

The Catalan-Gothic church of Sant Joan Baptista looks almost Arabic, guarded by palm trees and a tall, square bell-tower linked to the main church by a tiny bridge. Rebuilt in the 16th century, it has a colourful rose window over the west door. Another church, the convent of Santa Anna, used to stage fights between bulls and bulldogs, and bullfights can still be seen at the Plaça de Toros, built out of white stone in its own quarry in 1910.

Sa Pobla, 4km north of Muro, is Mallorca's vegetable basket; this fertile area of marshes reclaimed as farmland is referred to as 'the land of a thousand windmills'. It is also the home of one of Mallorca's most unusual festivals, the Revelta de Sant Antoni. For two days each January pets are led through the town to be blessed outside the church, dancers drive out the Devil for the coming year, and everyone eats pastries filled with spicy spinach and marsh eels.

ORIENT ⭐⭐

Nervous drivers should not even think about tackling the 10-km hairpin road to Orient from Bunyola (there is a much easier approach from Alaró). But those who make it to this village are rewarded with a marvellous sight – one of Mallorca's tiniest hamlets, with a population of less than 30, nestling among olive trees at the foot of Puig d'Alfábia. Orient is popular with walkers – numerous walks start from here, including an ascent to Castell d'Alaró – and with weekend day trippers from Palma, who visit its three restaurants for Sunday lunch.

PALMA NOVA ⭐

There are people who can remember when this was just a village; then along came the tourist boom, and 'new Palma' became the favoured resort of the British. More restrained than Magaluf, less exclusive than Portals Nous, Palma Nova occupies a prime position on the western side of the bay of Palma. It makes a good base for a family holiday, with nearby attractions including Marineland and Aquapark (▶ 108, 109) – as long as you don't mind sharing your family holiday with a thousand others.

PEGUERA ⭐

This beach resort, popular with German tour operators, was the first in Mallorca to have its own artificial beach. Once on the main road from Palma to Andratx, it has become much more peaceful since the construction of a bypass and the opening of a seafront promenade. Just outside Peguera is Cala Fornells, a chic resort of terracotta houses set around a pretty cove. Nearby Camp de Mar is a fast-growing resort where racing driver Michael Schumacher and model Claudia Schiffer both have homes.

✚ 28C4
🍴 Three good restaurants (££)
↔ Castell d'Alaró (▶ 19)

Orient is a favourite spot for mountain walkers, cyclists and lovers of Mallorcan cuisine

✚ 28B3
🍴 Wide choice of restaurants (£–££)
🚌 Regular buses from Palma
↔ Magaluf (▶ 59), Portals Nous (▶ 72)

✚ 28B3
🍴 Wide choice of restaurants (£–££)
🚌 From Palma

The house in Petra where Junípero Serra was born has been preserved much as it would have been in the 18th century

🔲 29D3
🍴 Es Celler restaurant (££); bars on main square (£)
🚌 From Palma
↔️ Ermita de Bonany (▶ 55)
❓ Market held Wed

Serra House and Museum
✉️ Carrer Barracar Alt
☎️ 971 561149
🕐 By arrangement – follow the directions to the keyholder's house
✋ Donation requested

🔲 73C2
🍴 Wide choice of bars and restaurants (£–££)
🚌 Regular buses from Palma

PETRA

This sleepy town of sand-coloured houses would be completely off the tourist map if it were not the birthplace of Mallorca's most famous son, Fray Junípero Serra. Born in 1713, he became a priest in 1730 and worked as a missionary in Mexico from 1749 to 1763. At the age of 54 he was sent to California; the missions he established there grew into some of the USA's largest cities, including San Diego and San Francisco.

You can visit the **house** where Serra's parents lived, a **museum** devoted to his life and work, the font where he was baptised (in the church of Sant Pere) and a plaque, outside the same church, describing him as 'explorer, missionary, hero, civiliser'. Anyone walking down the street leading to his birthplace, decorated with majolica tiles depicting him baptising Native Americans, might be inclined to disagree, but by the standards of his day he was certainly a hero.

PLATJA DE PALMA ✪

If you cannot wait to get on a beach, this 5-km stretch of fine white sand is just minutes from the airport. The two resorts of Can Pastilla and S'Arenal have merged into one, connected by a long palm-lined promenade offering every possible entertainment in summer. This is a good resort for families – there are children's playgrounds and a miniature train ride, though the nightlife can get a bit raucous. Take a *passeig* here before dinner and you have a fabulous view of Palma, the twinkling lights on the waterfront reflected in the sea.

The Central Plain

This lovely drive criss-crosses the central plain, following old Roman roads through almond and apricot groves on its way to several small market towns.

Start in Petra, following signs to Santa Margalida from the parish church. Bypass Santa Margalida by bearing left towards Muro.

In Muro (▶ 62), Carrer Major takes you to the museum – well worth a visit.

Continue along Carrer Major, over a crossroads and past the church of Sant Joan Baptista towards Sa Pobla.

Next you cross a fertile land of windmills, red earth and potato fields. Up ahead you see the mountains.

Skirting Sa Pobla, follow the signs to Llubi; go uphill into the village and down again to reach a main road, where you turn left and immediately right towards Sineu.

Drystone walls to either side line the route to Sineu (▶ 86). As you approach Sineu, turn left at the crossroads (signposted to Sant Joan) to pass underneath a modern sculpture outside the S'Estació art gallery.

Continue towards Sant Joan. Before reaching the village, turn right to Montuïri (▶ 60).

Bypassing Montuïri, cross the Palma–Manacor highway by the Orquídea pearl shop and head for Porreres (▶ 67). A short detour takes you up to the Santuari de Montesió.

Leave Porreres in the direction of Vilafranca de Bonany (▶ 90). Turn left in Vilafranca and pass Els Calderers on your right.

You could visit the stately home of Els Calderers, taking a short cut to Sant Joan.

Take the next right turn to Sant Joan, from where you can return to Petra.

There are excellent views of the Ermita de Bonany and of Petra's church as you approach.

Distance
81km

Time
3 hours

Start/end point
Petra
✛ 29D3

Lunch
Centro (£)
✉ Avinguda Bisbe Campins, Porreres
☎ 971 168372

Climbing the Calvari steps on the way to salvation, with Puig de Maria in the background

🔲 29D5
🍴 Excellent cafés and restaurants (££)
🚌 From Palma
🔄 Cala de Sant Vicenç (► 47), Port de Pollença (► 70), Puig de Maria (► 74)
❓ Market held Sun; classical music festival, Jul–Sep; *Devallement* procession, Good Fri; *Moros i Cristians*, mock battle, 2 Aug

Museu de Pollença
☎ 971 531166
🕐 Tue–Sun 11–1
💰 Cheap

POLLENÇA   ✪✪✪

At the eastern end of the Serra de Tramuntana and tucked between two hills, each topped by a sacred site, Pollença is the perfect Mallorcan town. Large enough to avoid being twee but small enough to wander round in a morning, it has none of the feel of other towns which have succumbed under the sheer weight of tourism. Foreigners have long been attracted here, but Pollença has learned to accept and adapt to tourism without losing its soul. Café life is still the rule; if you want to join in, come on a Sunday morning when the Plaça Major is filled with market stalls and the locals congregate after church to relax in the Café Espanyol.

The Pont Romà (Roman bridge) on the edge of town gives a clue to Pollença's long history. The name Pollença dates from the 14th century, when settlers from Alcúdia named the town after their former Roman capital. Among many historic buildings is a former Jesuit convent, now the town hall. From here you climb 365 steps, lined with cypress trees, to reach the Calvari church, with its ancient wooden cross and views of Puig de Maria (► 74). The Calvari steps are the scene of a moving procession each Good Friday, when a figure of Christ is removed from a cross and carried down the steps by torchlight.

The **municipal museum** in the former Dominican convent contains the remains of prehistoric sculptures shaped like bulls, as well as a *mandala* (Tibetan sand painting) given by the Dalai Lama in 1990. The cloisters of the convent are the venue for Pollença's celebrated classical music festival.

PORRERES ★

Porreres is typical of the small towns on the Mallorcan plain – nothing much to see, but an easy-going atmosphere and a good place to while away a couple of hours. The main street, Avinguda Bisbe Campins, runs from the church to the town hall and is lined with bars and cafés. Inside the town hall is a small modern **art gallery** with two works by Salvador Dalí. Just outside Porreres is a former hilltop hermitage, **Santuari de Montesió**, with a simple chapel, irregular cloisters and views across the plain and out to sea. You can stay here in very basic rooms.

- 🚹 29D3
- ☎ Art gallery: 971 647221; Sanctuary: 971 647185
- 🕐 Art gallery: Tue 10:30–12:30
- 🍴 Choice of restaurants and bars (£)
- 💷 Art gallery: free
- ❓ Market held Tue

PORT D'ALCÚDIA ★

As the name suggests, this was once just a port serving a city – now the port has completely outgrown the town that it serves. The biggest of the resorts on Mallorca's northeast coast, it stands at the head of a 10-km stretch of sandy beach which continues around the bay of Alcúdia as far as Can Picafort. The area around the fishing harbour is the most attractive; the promenade on Passeig Marítim faces a row of fish restaurants. Near here is the commercial port, where passenger ferries leave for the Menorcan city of Ciutadella.

- 🚹 29D5
- 🍴 Wide choice of restaurants (££)
- 🚌 From Palma and Alcúdia; also from Port de Pollença in summer
- 🔁 Alcúdia (► 16)

PORT D'ANDRATX ★★

Dress up to come here, or you will feel seriously out of place. Port d'Andratx is one of Mallorca's classiest resorts, popular with the yachting fraternity and with film stars whose Italian-style villas can be seen climbing up the hillsides. But don't let that put you off; come here all the same. The harbour is one of the prettiest in Mallorca and a table at one of the waterside bars is really the perfect place to watch the sunset.

- 🚹 28A3
- 🍴 Wide choice of restaurants (££–£££)
- 🚌 From Andratx
- 🔁 Andratx (► 43)

Port d'Andratx, where the yachting set like to meet

Food & Drink

Mallorcan cuisine, based on pork, fish and vegetables with generous use of garlic and olive oil, is hearty peasant fare steeped in tradition and rooted in local ingredients.

Good *Tapas*

- *Datiles con bacon* – dates wrapped in bacon
- *Mejillones relleñas* – stuffed mussels
- *Pimientos de Padrón* – small chillies deep-fried with salt
- *Pulpo gallego* – Galician-style octopus with olive oil
- *Tortilla española* – cold potato omelette

Not long ago every village would celebrate the *matança*, the winter slaughter of pigs, with songs and dancing and the making of hams and sausages for the coming year. Sausages come in several varieties – *sobrasada* (raw minced pork with hot red pepper) and *botifarró* (cured pork with blood), as well as spicy *chorizo* from Spain. And no bar would be complete without its *jamón serrano*, a whole cured ham displayed on an attractive slicing-board.

Mallorcan Specialities

A side effect of the *matança* was *frit mallorquí*, a fry-up of the most perishable offal with potatoes, onions and tomatoes. Nowadays you find it on menus alongside *tumbet*, a Mallorcan-style ratatouille of aubergines, potatoes and peppers in olive oil, and *sopes mallorquines*, a thick broth of thinly-sliced brown bread and vegetables. Other classic dishes include *llom amb col* (pork wrapped in cabbage with pine nuts and raisins) and *lechona asada* (roast suckling pig).

Paella is not a Mallorcan dish but it is widely available; *paella ciega* (blind man's *paella*) comes without bones. The local equivalent is *arròs brut* ('dirty rice'), saffron rice cooked with chicken, pork and vegetables. Fish is mostly imported and frozen – restaurants have to state this – but lobster, prawns, sardines and sea bass are all good. The latter, baked in rock salt, is a Mallorcan speciality.

Desserts are not Mallorca's strong point – often the choice is between *helado* (ice cream) and *flan* (crème caramel). An interesting alternative is *gato de almendras*, almond cake served with toasted almond ice cream. Mallorcans are very proud of *ensaimadas*, fluffy,

spiral-shaped pastries dusted with sugar and filled with anything from pumpkin jam to *sobrasada* sausage; the secret ingredient is said to be the lard in the pastry. Cheeses include Mahón from Menorca and Manchego from central Spain as well as local varieties.

Sobrasada *sausages (above) and* ensaimadas *(left) are treated with a reverence normally reserved for works of art*

Wine

The *vi* or *vino de la casa* will probably be Mallorcan, but most bottled wine is imported from Spain. The best red wines come from La Rioja – wine labelled *crianza* is aged in oak for at least a year, *reserva* for two, *gran reserva* for three. Penedés red and white wines from Catalunya are good value; Cava, Spanish sparkling wine, is from the same area. But don't disparage Mallorcan wines – the best stand comparison with anything at the same cost from mainland Spain (➤ 107).

Other Alcoholic Drinks

Spanish and imported beer (*cerveza*) are available everywhere – for draught beer, ask for *una caña*. Sherry is always *fino* – dry and chilled. Spanish brandy (*coñac*) comes in a bewildering variety of bottles and is added to coffee at any time of day. Leading brands include Fundador, Magno and Soberano. Gin is manufactured on Menorca – ask for Xoriguer brand. Local liqueurs include *hierbas secos* (dry) and *hierbas dulces* (sweet), both based on aniseed and packed full of herbs.

Soft Drinks

Tap water is safe but everyone drinks mineral water – *con gas* is sparkling, *sin gas* is still. Freshly squeezed orange juice (*zumo de naranja*) is refreshing and delicious, as are summer *granizados* (fruit slushes) of orange or lemon. An unusual local drink is *orxata* or *horchata*, almond milk. *Café solo* is a small shot of strong black coffee; *café con leche* comes with hot milk. If you want something less stimulating, ask for *manzanilla* (camomile) or *poliomenta* (peppermint tea).

PORT DE POLLENÇA ✪✪

This genteel, old-fashioned resort at the mouth of Pollença bay is particularly popular with families, and with older visitors in winter. There is also a large community of foreign residents, mostly retired British. The promenade along Passeig Voramar, all whitewashed villas and pine trees leaning into the sea, is perfect for an early evening walk. Look out for the bust of Hermen Anglada-Camarasa, the Catalan painter who spent many years in Pollença and whose work is displayed in the Fundació la Caixa in Palma (► 33). A favourite walk from Port de Pollença is the 3-km hike across the Formentor peninsula through the Bóquer valley, a paradise for ornithologists and lovers of wild flowers.

> ### Did you know ?
>
> Port de Pollença has long been the favoured resort of the British middle classes, who would stay at its water-front hotels enjoying casual flirtations and games of bowls on the beach. The British crime writer Agatha Christie captures this world in a 1936 short story, Problem at Pollensa Bay.

PORT DE SÓLLER ✪✪

This small resort, set around a fish-shaped natural harbour, has the only beach of any note along the entire north coast. It is the starting-point for several boat trips along the coast; the trip to Sa Calobra (► 78) is one of the few to run throughout the year. Port de Sóller is also a good base for walks. A climb of less than an hour brings you to Cap Gros lighthouse for panoramic views of the bay and the mountains behind; a longer path, through rock gardens and olive groves, connects with an old mule track from Deià to Sóller.

A Day Out by Train & Tram

The opening of a railway line from Palma to Sóller in 1912, and a tram linking Sóller to its port the following year, brought the northwest coast within easy reach of the capital. The vintage carriages are still in use, providing a joyride for tourists and a relief for locals from the terrors of the Palma–Sóller road. Five trains a day leave from Plaça d'Espanya in Palma – the 10:40 is labelled the *turístico* but all you get for the extra cost is a more crowded train and a short photo stop.

The train, all mahogany panels and brass fittings, leaves Palma amid a bustle of hisses, hoots and whistles before rattling down the city streets and into the suburbs.

Time
1½ hours each way

Start point
Plaça d'Espanya, Palma
35D4
Most city buses terminate here; island buses terminate near by

End point
Port de Sóller
28C5

Lunch
Tapas bars (£)
Plaça Constitució, Sóller

Soon you are out on the plain, passing small country stations and pigs rooting beneath the trees. If you feel like a break, you can get off at Bunyola and climb up the hill to reach the centre of this sleepy village, with cafés on the main square.

Stay on the train and soon you start to climb, entering a 3-km tunnel before returning to daylight for the drop, through a dizzying series of bends, to Sóller (► 86).

The 'Orange Express' tram to Port de Sóller runs hourly, connecting with the arrival of the train. Stand on the platform as it clatters through orchards and back gardens and you can imagine you are living 50 years earlier.

It takes 20 minutes to complete the 5-km journey to the port. If you do not want to return the same way, buses leave from the jetty for Palma via Deià and Valldemossa.

Take the toytown train from Palma to Sóller (above), then hop on a tram to its port (left)

71

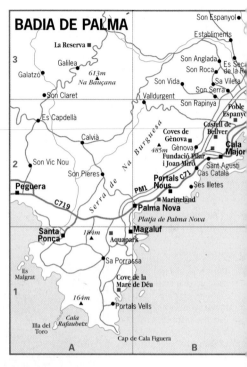

BADIA DE PALMA

Son Espanyol
Establiments
La Reserva ■
3
Galilea
Galatzó •
613m
Na Bâuçana
Son Anglada Es Sec
Son Roca de la R
Son Vida Sa Vileta
Son Serra
Son Claret
Son Rapinya Poble
Espany(
Es Capdellà
Castell de
Bellver
Coves de
Gènova ■
485m Gènova •
Cala
Major
Calvià
Na Burguesa
Fundació Pilar
i Joan Miró
Sant Agusti
2
Son Vic Nou
Son Pieres
Serra de
Portals C71
Nous
Cas Català
Ses Illetes
PM1
Peguera
C719
Marineland
Palma Nova
Platja de Palma Nova
Santa
Ponça
184m
Magaluf
Aquapark
Es
Malgrat
Sa Porrassa
Cove de la
Mare de Déu
1
164m
Portals Vells
Illa del
Toro
Cala
Rafaubetx
Cap de Cala Figuera
A
B

72B2
Wide choice of bars and restaurants (££–£££)
21 from Palma
Palma Nova (➤ 63), Ses Illetes (➤ 85)

28B3
Beach bar and restaurant (££)
From Palma Oct–May, Mon–Fri (☎ 971 717190)

PORTALS NOUS ✪

This is one of the more exclusive resorts in the bay of Palma – not many high-rise hotels here, just rows of private villas and apartments dominating the shoreline. Puerto Portals marina, opened in 1987, is the summer home of the jet set. King Juan Carlos has been known to moor here while staying at his summer palace, Marivent, in nearby Cala Major, and the younger royals can be seen frequenting the waterfront restaurants and bars. Don't even think about looking in the smart boutiques unless you have a high credit card limit.

PORTALS VELLS ✪✪

A bumpy track from Magaluf leads through pine woods to this beautiful cove at the southwest tip of Palma bay. In summer it gets crowded, but out of season you could have your own private beach, with golden sand, rocky cliffs and shimmering turquoise water. In fact there are two beaches; the smaller one, El Mago, is Mallorca's official nudist beach. From the main beach, hike along the cliffs to the Cove de la Mare de Déu, a rock chapel built by fishermen to give thanks for a safe landing. Back on the road, another 2km brings you to the headland of Cap de

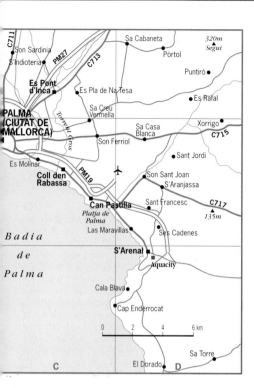

Cala Figuera, where you look back at sweeping views of the entire bay of Palma.

How the other half lives – the glitzy marina at Puerto Portals looks across the water to the mass-market resorts at Palma Nova and Magaluf

73

PORTO COLOM ★

29E2
Choice of restaurants (££)
From Palma and Felanitx

This fishing village, once the port for Felanitx, was named in honour of Christopher Columbus, who is said – without much evidence – to have been born here. Until the late 19th century Porto Colom was busy supplying wine to France; but when phylloxera killed the vines, its role as a port diminished and it has only recently discovered a new life as a tourist resort. Popular with Mallorcan and Spanish visitors and set inside a deep natural harbour, it still has the feel of a small fishing port with boats around the quay and pastel-coloured houses lining the waterfront, each with its own landing stage. Cala Marçal, 2km south, has a wide sandy beach leading to a narrow rocky cove.

PORTO CRISTO ★

29E3
Wide choice of restaurants (££)
From Palma and Manacor
Coves del Drac and Coves dels Hams (▶ 54)
Market held Sun

This was one of the main resorts on the east coast until Cala Millor came along. So much the better: with bigger and better beaches elsewhere, Porto Cristo has carved out a role as a friendly, family resort, taking advantage of a superb position at the end of a long, sheltered inlet. Once the port for Manacor, Porto Cristo was the only place in Mallorca to be caught up in the Spanish Civil War, when it was briefly captured by Republican forces in 1936. There is not much to do but swim, sunbathe and dine at the terrace restaurants which are perfectly placed to catch the lunchtime sun – but day trippers come in droves to visit the nearby caves (▶ 54). Other nearby family attractions include an aquarium and a safari park (▶ 108, 109).

PÒRTOL ★

28C4
Bars (£)
From Palma
Market held Thu; Fira del Fang, annual pottery fair held in Mar in the nearby town of Marratxi

The neighbouring villages of Pòrtol and Sa Cabaneta, between Palma and Santa Maria del Camí, have become something of an artists' colony. Unlike in Deià and Banyalbufar, though, the artists are Mallorcan – potters taking advantage of the rich local soil. The only reason for coming here is to visit the *ollerías* (workshops), where prices are much lower than in the tourist shops. Good buys include *greixoneras* (heavy earthenware cooking pots) and *ollas* (clay storage jars), as well as simple brown-glazed plates and *plats morenos*, glazed bowls painted with symbols (some of the designs go back to Arab times). Several artists specialise in the clay whistles called *siurells*.

PUIG DE MARIA ★★

29D5
971 184132
Bar-restaurant (£)
From Palma to Pollença
Free
Pollença (▶ 66)

Climb for an hour out of Pollença, or drive up a terrifying potholed road, and you are rewarded with views over Cap de Formentor and the entire northeastern coast – as well as back down over Pollença. Nuns settled on Puig de Maria ('Mary's mountain') in 1371 and remained for several hundred years, refusing to leave even when the Bishop of Palma ordered them down for their own safety. The convent is still there, on top of the mountain; the chapel smells of incense and the refectory of woodsmoke. You can stay in simple cells in the sanctuary here, but don't expect luxury – you pay extra if you take a shower. The caretaker will rustle up a *paella* to save you the long walk back to town.

PUIG DE RANDA ✪✪✪

This table mountain, rising 543m out of the plain, has been a place of pilgrimage ever since Ramón Llull (► 14) founded Mallorca's first hermitage here in 1275. He came aged 40, shaken by an incident which caused him to review his way of life. Bent on seduction he chased a married woman through Palma on horseback; unable to shake him off, she lifted her blouse to reveal cancerous breasts. Llull retired in isolation to Puig de Randa to ponder a life of youthful excess. These days pilgrims to Puig de Randa are as likely to be weekend cyclists in search of a challenge as seekers after religious truth. The winding road to the summit leads to three separate hermitages. The lowest, Oratori de Nostra Senyora de Gràcia, is perched on a ledge in the cliff above a sheer 200-m drop. Further up is the Santuari de Sant Honorat and finally Santuari de Cura, where Llull lived. The sense of history is somewhat offset by the radio mast on the mountain top and the electric candles in the church, but this is still a special place. Visit the Sala Gramàtica to see Llull's original manuscripts and a bottle of 1934 Chartreuse made in the monastery, then look out from the terrace at the views of the plain, with Palma Bay and the isle of Cabrera in the distance. Simple rooms are available in a modern pilgrims' block.

🕂 29D3
☎ 971 120260
🍴 Restaurant at Santuari de Cura (££)
✋ Free

Randa, the village at the foot of the mountain. The climb from here to the summit is one of Mallorca's most testing cycle rides

🔲 29F3

🍴 Snack bar (£)

🚌 From Palma to Cala Millor

👐 Free

↔ Cala Millor (➤ 48)

PUNTA DE N'AMER ⭐

This 200-hectare nature reserve on a headland jutting out from the east coast is an oasis of peace amid a desert of high-rise apartments and hotels. Once, the whole coast was like this – thankfully, environmentalists have saved this small section from development. Walk south from Cala Millor, or north from Sa Coma, on a well-defined 1.5-km track. Eventually you reach the Castell de n'Amer, a 17th-century watchtower. Have a drink at the summit and look down at what you have left behind.

How to go walking in the mountains without getting lost – follow the easy waymarked trail around La Reserva

🔲 28B3

☎ 971 616622

🕐 Apr–Sep, daily 10–7; Oct–Mar, daily 10–6

🍴 Café (£)

👐 Expensive

↔ Galilea (➤ 56)

LA RESERVA ⭐

On the slopes of Puig de Galatzó near the village of Puigpunyent, this nature reserve describes itself as 'Mallorca's paradise'. A 3-km trail of waymarked paths leads you through Mallorca's mountain scenery in less than two hours, past waterfalls and springs, olive trees and charcoal stoves. A series of boards provides background information on wildlife and mountain industries. Well laid out and interesting, the reserve gives you a feeling for the area. It will seem a bit sterile if you have been out in the mountains on your own – but it might help you to make sense of what you have already seen.

S'ALBUFERA ✪✪

Just off the coast road 5km south of Port d'Alcúdia, the S'Albufera wetlands make a welcome relief from long stretches of crowded beach. Birdwatchers come from all over Europe to see rare migrants like Montagu's harriers and Eleanora's falcons; species breeding here include stonechats, moustached warblers and the long-eared owl. Ospreys leave their breeding sites on the cliffs to come here to fish; peregrines and hoopoes live here all year round.

The name derives from the Arabic for 'lagoon', but the site has been exploited since Roman times – Pliny writes of night herons, probably from S'Albufera, being sent to Rome as a gastronomic delicacy. The wetlands were drained for agriculture in the 19th century by a British company which subsequently went bankrupt; the network of canals dates from this time. Rice was introduced in the early 20th century, paper was manufactured from the reeds and sedge, and it is only since 1985, following fears that tourist development was damaging the area's fragile ecology, that S'Albufera has been a protected nature reserve. There are footpaths, cycle trails, birdwatching hides and an audio-visual display room where you can listen to birdsong.

🕂 29D4
✉ Carretera Port d'Alcúdia–Artà, km5
☎ 971 892250
🕐 Apr–Sep, daily 9–7; Oct–Mar, daily 9–5
🍴 Picnic area
🚌 From Port d'Alcúdia to Cala Rajada in summer
💷 Free
❓ Cars are not allowed in the reserve – leave them 1km from the visitor centre on the main road in the car park opposite Hotel Parc Natural

Get away from it all with a day at S'Albufera, walking among the marshes and listening to the birds

+ 28C5
🍴 Several restaurants
(£–££)
🚢 From Port de Sóller (all
year ☎ 971 633109)
? Choral concert on the
beach in Jul (☎ 971
171958)

SA CALOBRA ⭐⭐

Do not believe anyone who tells you that they have discovered the perfect unspoilt cove on the north coast – at least, not if its name is Sa Calobra. This is indeed a beautiful spot, which is why tour buses pour in by the dozen every day, even in winter.

The journey to Sa Calobra is as memorable as the bay itself. A twisting road around Puig Major plunges 800m in just 12km, turning 270 degrees at one point to loop under itself (a feature known as the 'Knotted Tie'). The easier approach is by boat from Port de Sóller, passing genuinely isolated bays with an excellent view of Puig Major, albeit spoilt by the military installations on the summit of Mallorca's highest mountain.

Once there, walk through 200m of tunnels to reach the Torrent de Pareis ('twin streams'), which begins several kilometres up in the mountains at the confluence of the torrents of Lluc and Gorg Blau. Up to 400m high and only 30m wide, with some sections never seeing daylight, this dramatic gorge culminates in a small pebble beach where you can picnic among the crowds. In summer, when the gorge is dry, you can hike inland between the cliffs; do not attempt this in winter.

A side turn off the road to Sa Calobra leads to Cala Tuent, a small cove with a sandy beach and a 13th-century church, Ermita de Sant Llorenç. Cala Tuent is likely to be quieter than Sa Calobra; but don't believe anyone who tells you they have discovered the *real* unspoilt cove...

View through a rock arch at Sa Calobra – Mallorca's most beautiful spot, or a place spoilt by tourists?

SA DRAGONERA ✪

This uninhabited island off Mallorca's western tip was the focus for a turning point in Mallorcan history in 1977, when it was occupied by environmentalists protesting against a planned tourist development. The campaigners won, the island became a nature reserve instead, the seabirds survived, and for the first time the authorities realised that mass tourism had reached its limit.

Six kilometres long and crowned by an ancient watchtower, Sa Dragonera takes its name from its shape, said to resemble a dragon. You can visit in summer by boat from Sant Elm; in winter you have to make do with views of the dragon from the beach at Sant Elm or from the climb to Sa Trapa (▶ below).

🔲 28A3
🚏 From Sant Elm Mar–Oct
(☎ 971 757065)
↔ Sant Elm (▶ below)

From Sant Elm you can climb to an abandoned monastery or take a boat to Sa Dragonera

SANT ELM ✪✪

The main reason for visiting Sant Elm, a laid-back resort with a fine sandy beach, is for the views of Sa Dragonera (▶ above). You can take a boat to the island from the jetty at the end of the main street, or sit outside the fish restaurants on the same jetty.

A challenging walk from Sant Elm leads to the abandoned Trappist monastery of Sa Trapa. Set out on Avinguda de la Trapa and climb through coastal *maquis* and pine, with fine views of Sa Dragonera. The round trip takes about three hours; a shorter route is signposted beside the cemetery on the Sant Elm to Andratx road. Near here is the village of S'Arracó, built by Spanish settlers returning from the American colonies.

🔲 28A3
🍴 Choice of restaurants
(££)
🚌 From Andratx or Peguera
🚆 From Port d'Andratx and Peguera in summer
↔ Sa Dragonera (▶ above)

28C4
Local bars (£)
One or two buses daily
from Palma
Market held Sat

Natura Parc
Carretera de Sineu, km15
971 144078
Daily 10–7
Expensive

28C4
Bars and cafés (£)
From Palma and Inca
Market held Sun

28B3
Bars and restaurants
(£–££)
From Palma
Rei en Jaume regatta
in Jul

SANTA EUGÈNIA ✪

People argue over whether the mountains or the coast represent 'the real Mallorca', but the heart of the island is to be found in villages like this, surrounded by farmland with views to the sierra where the mountains rise out of the plain. The 6-km cart track to the neighbouring village of Sencelles offers good walking, and there is also the climb to Puig de Santa Eugènia (► 81). Natura Parc, on the edge of the village, is a popular family attraction with nature trails and indigenous farm animals as well as a butterfly garden.

SANTA MARIA DEL CAMÍ ✪

This market town on the Palma–Inca railway has developed a reputation as one of Mallorca's artistic centres. Most of the island's potters work close by, in Pòrtol (► 74), and Santa Maria is the centre of manufacture of *roba de llengues* ('cloth of tongues'), cotton woven into bright zigzag patterns and used in curtains, bedspreads and upholstery. Just off the main square is Ca'n Conrado, former Carmelite cloisters and a peaceful retreat from the traffic on the Palma road.

SANTA PONÇA ✪

Santa Ponça may look like just another beach resort but it has a permanent place in Mallorcan history. It was here that Jaume I landed in 1229 to begin his conquest of Mallorca, a conquest he described as 'the best thing man has done for a hundred years past'. A relief on a large cross above the marina, erected in 1929, records the event.

A Walk from Santa Eugènia

This simple walk gives spectacular views for the minimum of effort.

Leave the village of Santa Eugènia and head in the direction of Santa Maria del Camí. After 1km turn left along a narrow lane to Ses Coves.

The lane bends left, then descends, and you see Ses Coves ('the caves'), used at various times as pirate hideaways and wine cellars. One of them still contains an ancient winepress.

When the road divides, fork left; after five minutes you reach some iron gates at the entrance to a track on your right.

Here you have an optional detour to the summit of Puig d'En Marron, adding about an hour to your walk. Step over the low wall beside the iron gates, and climb until the road runs out. Continue along a mud track through the pine woods, keeping right at each fork, until you emerge onto a wide open plateau with wonderful views. Return to the iron gates by the same route and turn right to rejoin the main walk.

Follow the lane briefly uphill; when the lane divides, take the track on the left. After passing an arched entrance to a well, turn immediately left through an orchard towards a house. To the right of the house, the wall is marked with a red dot; climb from here to a pass.

Here you can clamber over a stone wall to your left to reach the cross on the summit of Puig de Santa Eugènia. This is the high point of the walk, with wonderful views that stretch across the plain to the mountains in the distance. On the opposite clifftop is one of Mallorca's oddest sights – the cockpit of a broken-up plane.

Retrace your steps to the stone wall and then follow the path that leads through the bushes on your left to return to Santa Eugènia.

Distance
4.5km (optional detour adds 3km)

Time
1–2 hours

Start/end point
Santa Eugènia
✚ 28C4
🚌 From Palma – only one or two buses per day, so check timetable

Lunch
Ca Na Cantona (£)
✉ Carrer Balenguera, Santa Eugènia
☎ 971 144031

SANTANYÍ

Do not be surprised if the buildings in Santanyí look just that little bit more mellow than everywhere else – this small town is the source of the golden sandstone used in Palma's cathedral and La Llotja among others. The old gate, Sa Porta Murada, seen as you enter the town from Palma, is a good example of Santanyí stone and a reminder that this was once a walled town. The parish church of Sant Andreu Apòstel contains a massive rococo organ, designed by Jordi Bosch and brought here from a convent in Palma. The streets around the church are the focus for one of Mallorca's liveliest markets.

■ 29E2
▮▮ Bars and cafés (£)
🚌 From Palma and Cala Figuera
↔ Cala Figuera (► 47), Ses Salines (► 85)
❓ Market held Wed, Sat; Sant Andreu *festa*, 30 Nov

SANTUARI DE SANT SALVADOR ✪✪

This old hermitage, 509m above sea level at the highest point of the Serra de Llevant, was the senior house of Mallorca's monastic order and the last to lose its monks, in 1992. It is still a popular place of pilgrimage, flanked by two enormous landmarks – to one side a 14-m stone cross, to the other a 35-m column topped by a statue of Christ holding out his right hand in blessing. The church contains a fine carved alabaster retable, but more interesting is the side chapel off the gatehouse, full of poignant mementos

■ 29E3
✉ Signposted from Felanitx–Porto Colom road
☎ 971 827282
▮▮ Bar-restaurant (£) and picnic tables
🖐 Free
↔ Felanitx (► 55)

The views from the Santuari de Sant Salvador stretch right across the central plain

and prayers to Our Lady. Like other former monasteries, Sant Salvador has a few simple rooms available for pilgrims.

The views from the terrace take in Cabrera, Cap de Formentor and several other hilltop sanctuaries dotted across the plain. From the statue of Christ you look out towards the Castell de Santueri, a 14th-century rock castle built into the cliffs on the site of a ruined Arab fortress.

SERRA DE TRAMUNTANA ✪✪✪

The 'mountains of the north wind' which run the length of Mallorca's north coast are home to the island's most spectacular landscapes. Pine-covered slopes almost lean into the sea; as you climb higher, forested hills give way to barren crags and peaks. The people of Mallorca have good reason to be grateful to the mountains. In winter they act as a buffer, shielding the plain from the fierce *tramuntana* wind and absorbing most of the island's rain and snow; in summer they provide a cool retreat from the heat of Palma and the south.

The Serra de Tramuntana runs for 88km from Andratx to Pollença, with the rocky outcrops of Sa Dragonera and Cap de Formentor at either end. Of the ten peaks over

Fresh air, walking and sea views – the Serra de Tramuntana mountains (above) and Cap de Ses Salines (right)

1,000m, most are concentrated in the area around Lluc; the highest are Puig Major (1,445m) and Puig Massanella (1,349m). There are no rivers, though there are several mountain torrents which swell rapidly after rain – and the Cúber and Gorg Blau reservoirs, essential resources on an island so often affected by drought.

The mountains are best seen slowly, on foot; you smell the wild rosemary, hear the sheep-bells, frighten the goats, breathe in the air and marvel at pine trees growing out of red rock, a divine version of the colours of Mallorcan village houses. If you have to drive, take care – the roads here are the most dangerous on the island, and the endless procession of hairpin bends requires total concentration. The most dramatic drive of all is the C710 from Sóller to Lluc, traversing tunnels and gorges on its way between Puig Major and Puig Massanella.

SES COVETES ✪

The name of this village means 'small caves' and this is believed to refer to Roman burial chambers on the same site. Nowadays people come here for one thing – to get to Platja Es Trenc, a 3-km stretch of fine white sand backed by gentle dunes. This has long been an unofficial nudist beach, even during the puritanical Franco era. It no longer has the hippy atmosphere of old, but it still makes a peaceful, less commercial contrast to some of the other beaches on the south coast.

➕ 29D2
🚌 From Palma, Jul–Aug, 3 times a day

SES ILLETES ✪

This genteel resort, with its white villas and old-fashioned hotels, is for many people the most attractive in the whole Badia de Palma. Two small beaches look out over a pair of *illetes* (islets), the larger one crowned by an old watch-tower. Its proximity to Palma means that you will never be alone here; in summer the buses from Palma to Ses Illetes are packed out at weekends. But if you want a base near the capital, combining a city break with a beach holiday, this could be just the place.

🞢 72B2
🍴 Cafés and restaurants (££)
🚌 3 from Palma
🔁 Portals Nous (▶ 72)

SES PAÏSSES ✪

Although not as extensive as the ruins at Capocorb Vell (▶ 50), this Bronze Age settlement near Artà is still a significant site and a link with Mallorcans of 3,000 years ago. Most impressive of all is the massive entrance portal, formed from three stone slabs weighing up to eight tonnes each. Inside there are several rooms and an *atalaia* (watchtower); the entire settlement is surrounded by a Cyclopean drystone wall.

🞢 29E4
🕐 Apr–Sep, daily 9–1, 3–7; Oct–Mar, Mon–Fri 9–1, 2:30–5, Sat 9–1
🚌 From Cala Rajada or Palma then a short walk
🖐 Cheap
🔁 Artà (▶ 45)

SES SALINES ✪

This small town between Santanyí and Colònia de Sant Jordi is named after the nearby saltpans, which act as a magnet for migrant waders and wildfowl on their way from Africa to their breeding grounds in Europe each spring. Cap de Ses Salines, Mallorca's southernmost point, is another good spot for birdwatching. The town itself makes a pleasant place to stroll, with an abundance of local Santanyí sandstone which turns golden in the sun. Just outside Ses Salines, on the road to Santanyí, is **Botanicactus**, one of Europe's largest botanical gardens, with bamboo and palm trees and, extraordinarily diverse in form, dozens of varieties of cactus.

🞢 29D2
🍴 Bars and cafés (£)
🚌 Between Colònia de Sant Jordi and Santanyí
🔁 Colònia de Sant Jordi (▶ 51), Santanyí (▶ 82)
❓ Market held Thu

Botanicactus
✉ Carretera Ses Salines–Santanyí, km1
☎ 971 649494
🕐 Apr–Sep, daily 9–7; Oct–Mar, daily 10–6
🖐 Moderate

SINEU ✪✪✪

29D4

🍴 Several restaurants (££)

❓ Market held Wed

S'Estació

✉ Carrer Estació 2

☎ 971 520750

🕐 Mon–Fri 9:30–1:30, 4–7, Sat 9–1

👐 Free

Sineu, at the geographical centre of Mallorca, comes alive each Wednesday morning at the island's most traditional market. It takes place on several levels. The sound of bleating leads you to the livestock market, where weather-beaten farmers haggle over the price of sheep before heading for the town's *celler* restaurants for an early brunch. Further up, on the way to the church, you pass the symbol of Sineu, a winged lion; near here are numerous stalls selling leather, lace and pearls. Eventually you reach Sa Plaça, the church square, where the action is liveliest of all, as local housewives turn out to buy the week's food. Buckets of olives, strings of tomatoes, bags of squirming snails – they are all here, along with plenty of fresh fruit, vegetables and flowers. Get to Sineu early, before the tour buses arrive, to catch the flavour of a traditional country market. Good buys include dried figs and apricots, pottery from Pòrtol and baskets from Sudan. Also in Sineu is S'Estació, an unusual modern art gallery based in the old station.

The winged lion, honouring St Mark, is the symbol of Sineu

SÓLLER ✪✪✪

28C4

🍴 Wide choice of bars and restaurants (£–££)

🚆 From Palma; tram to Port de Sóller

↔ Fornalutx (➤ 55), Port de Sóller (➤ 70)

❓ Market held Sat; *Moros i Cristians*, re-enactment of a 1561 battle in which local women helped to defeat a band of Turkish pirates, 8–10 May

Set in a lush valley of orange groves between the mountains and the sea, Sóller is popular with day trippers who arrive on the vintage train from Palma (➤ 71) and seem to do little but sit outside the cafés in Plaça Constitució soaking up the atmosphere and the sun. With several *tapas* bars, a fine selection of pastry shops, local ice cream and freshly squeezed orange juice, there is little temptation to move on.

Sóller grew rich on oranges and the results can be seen in its extravagant *modernista* architecture. The church of Sant Bartomeu has a 1912 arched tower suspended above the rose window, with spires like huge needles pointing

into the air. The same architect, Gaudí's pupil Joan Rubió, designed the Banco Central Hispano next door.

A stroll to the cemetery above the station, flanked by cypress trees and filled with potted plants, gives a clue to Sóller's history. Several of the epitaphs are in French, revealing the significant French community of the town, descendants of those who came to make their fortune by exporting oranges.

Sóller has two museums worth visiting. The **Natural Science Museum**, in a turn-of-the-19th-century manor house on the Palma road, has a collection of fossils and a botanical garden. The **Museu Municipal** is an 18th-century town house in the town centre, filled with antiques and relics of old Sóller.

A final word of advice: come here by train, rather than car. The climb over the Coll de Sóller, with its 57 hairpin bends, is the most terrifying drive in Mallorca. There is now a controversial new road tunnel through the mountain, but the train journey from Palma is a delight so why not give yourself a treat.

Sóller's main square (above) contains some interesting modern architecture, such as the bank designed by Joan Rubió (left)

Natural Science Museum
- ✉ Carretera Palma–Port de Sóller
- ☎ 971 634064
- 🕐 Apr–Sep, Tue–Sat 10–8, Sun 10:30–1:30; Oct–Mar, Tue–Sat 10–5:30, Sun 10:30–1:30
- 🖐 Cheap

Museu Municipal
- ✉ Currer del Mar 9
- ☎ 971 634663
- 🕐 Mon 11–5, Tue–Fri 10–6, Sat 10–2
- 🖐 Cheap

87

➕ 28B4
✉ Carretera Valldemossa–
  Deià
☎ 971 639158
🕐 Mon–Sat 9:30–2, 3–6
🍴 Mirador de Na Foradada
  (££)
🚌 From Palma,
  Valldemossa and Port de
  Sóller
💰 Cheap
↔ Deià (➤ 22)
❓ Sunset concerts in
  summer

SON MARROIG ⭐⭐

Of all the famous foreigners attracted to Mallorca's northwest coast, none is so admired locally as 'S'Arxiduc', Archduke Ludwig Salvator. Born in 1847 in the Pitti Palace, Florence, the son of Leopold III of Tuscany and Marie Antoinette de Bourbon, he came to Mallorca 20 years later to escape from Viennese court life and immediately fell in love with the island. An ecologist before it was fashionable, and an early hippy who wore Mallorcan peasant clothes, he bought up estates along the coast in an effort to save them from development, and devoted himself to studying and recording Mallorcan wildlife and traditions. His seven-volume *Las Baleares* took 20 years to produce and is still an authority on its subject. He died in 1915 in a Bohemian castle.

The Archduke's home at Son Marroig, outside Deià, has been turned into a shrine to his memory, with his photographs, paintings and books and a museum devoted to his life. In the gardens is a white marble rotunda, made from Carrara marble and imported from Italy, where you can sit and gaze at the Na Foradada ('pierced rock') peninsula, jutting out to sea with a gaping 18-m hole at its centre. Ask at the house for permission to walk onto the peninsula.

Private view – the Archduke's garden looks down over the peninsula of Na Foradada

Did you know ?

Another of the Archduke's estates, Miramar, was founded as a hermitage by Ramón Llull (➤ 14) in 1276. It has recently opened to the public – you can visit the library, see the collection of old maps and stroll around the gardens admiring the sea views. It is found close to Son Marroig on the road to Valldemossa.

VALLDEMOSSA (➤ 26, TOP TEN)

The Archduke's Bridlepath

This walk was mapped out by Archduke Ludwig Salvator during tours of his estates by mule; as well as spectacular coastal views, it gives an introduction to traditional mountain industries. You pass *sitjas* (round charcoal ovens), *casas de neu* (snow pits where winter snows were stored beneath a layer of ash), *forns de calç* (lime kilns) and *caças a coll* (thrush nets slung between the trees). The route is for experienced walkers only. Take food and water, a map, compass and whistle, and protection from sun, wind and rain. The weather on the mountains can change very quickly.

Begin at the car park opposite Bar Sa Mata on the main road through Valldemossa. Climb the hill behind the car park, towards the cemetery. Take the second right (Carrer Joan Fuster), then first left (Carrer de les Oliveres), continuing onto a rough track when the road runs out.

You climb gently at first, towards a group of pines, then more steeply, following red waymarks to a clearing. From here it is a short, tough climb to a mirador and the start of the Camí de S'Arxiduc, marked by a ruined stone refuge.

Follow the waymarks onto a high plateau and continue for about two hours.

For the best views of all, a one-hour diversion (just as the main path bears round to the right to begin its descent) takes you to the summit of the Teix, from where most of Mallorca is visible on a clear day.

The path drops back down to Valldemossa through a wooded valley, passing a shelter where you can camp in summer.

For a shorter walk to the foot of the Teix, you can simply do the final section in reverse. Leave Valldemossa by climbing past Son Gual, the large old house with a tower, seen just above the main road on the right as you enter from Palma (the path is signposted 'Teix-Refugi'. Turn left after 10 minutes onto a wide track. The climb through the valley to the shelter and back will take a couple of hours if you walk briskly.

Distance
13km

Time
6 hours

Start/end point
Valldemossa

 28B4
From Palma, Deià or Port de Sóller

Lunch
Take a picnic

🕂 29D3
🚌 From Palma and Manacor
❓ Market held Wed

Els Calderers
✉ Carretera Palma–
   Manacor, km37
☎ 971 526069
🕐 Apr–Sep, daily 10–6;
   Oct–Mar, daily 10–5
🍴 Café (£)
⬛ Moderate

*Vilafranca is famed for its
melons and sun-dried
tomatoes*

VILAFRANCA DE BONANY ✪

As you drive through this small town on the road from
Palma to Manacor, you cannot help noticing the strings of
vegetables hanging outside several of the shops –
peppers, aubergines, garlic and, above all, tomatoes.
These are the famous *tomàtigues de ramallet*, sold on
their stalks to be spread over *pa amb oli*. Vilafranca is also
known for its honeydew melons, whose harvest is
celebrated with a large melon festival each September.
The other reason for coming here, apart from food, is to
visit **Els Calderers**, a manor house between Vilafranca and
Sant Joan. This was once at the centre of a great wine
estate but like so many others it fell victim to the
phylloxera disease. Reopened in 1993, the 18th-century
house is now a museum of Mallorcan furniture and traditions; you can visit the wine cellar, granary, bakery, chapel
and wash-house as well as wander around the main house
with its paintings, guns and hunting trophies.

Where To...

Above: *Floorshow at Casino Mallorca;*
Right: *Wall plaque in Palma*

Palma

Prices
Prices are approximate, based on a three-course meal for one without drinks and service:

£ = under €12
££ = €12–24
£££ = over €24

Most restaurants serve a *menú del día* at lunchtime (▶ 96) which will usually work out much cheaper. It is normal practice to add about 10 per cent to the bill as a tip.

A Warning
Opening hours change frequently, and many restaurants take an annual holiday in winter. It is always a good idea to telephone before setting out.

Aramis (£££)
Modern Mediterranean cuisine and a weekly wine-tasting menu in a town house behind La Llotja.
✉ Carrer Montenegro 1 ☎ 971 725232 🕐 Lunch Mon–Fri, dinner Mon–Sat

Asador Tierra Asanda (££)
Barbecued and roasted meat – suckling pig, lamb, kid – in an old mansion close to Avinguda Jaume III.
✉ Carrer Concepció 4 ☎ 971 714256 🕐 Lunch Tue–Sat, dinner Mon–Sat

Baisakhi (££)
High-class Indian cuisine; try the gourmet menu, with wine and *lassi* included.
✉ Passeig Marítim 8 ☎ 971 736806 🕐 Lunch, dinner. Closed Mon

La Bodeguilla (££)
Classic Castilian stews amid hanging wine bottles; the same owners have a stylish *tapas* bar next door.
✉ Carrer Sant Jaume 1 and 3 ☎ 971 718274 🕐 Lunch, dinner. Closed Sun

Bon Lloc (£)
Vegetarian restaurant with good-value four-course set lunch.
✉ Carrer Sant Feliu 7 ☎ 971 718617 🕐 Lunch Mon–Sat, dinner Wed–Sat

Caballito de Mar (££)
Popular fish restaurant on the seafront.
✉ Passeig Sagrera 5 ☎ 971 721074 🕐 Lunch, dinner. Closed Mon

Ca'n Carlos (££)
One of the few restaurants in central Palma to focus on traditional Mallorcan cuisine.
✉ Carrer de l'Aigua 5 ☎ 971 713869 🕐 Lunch, dinner. Closed Sun

Candela (£££)
In a street better known for its *tapas* bars, this place offers fresh fish and creative Mediterranean cuisine.
✉ Carrer dels Apuntadors 14 ☎ 971 724428 🕐 Lunch, dinner. Closed Wed

Ca'n Eduardo (££)
Traditional fish restaurant above the fish market.
✉ Es Moll de Pescadors ☎ 971 721182 🕐 Lunch, dinner. Closed Sun

Ca'n Joan de S'Aigo (£)
Classy café where Joan Miró used to go for hot chocolate, almond ice cream and *ensaimadas*.
✉ Carrer Sant Sanç 10; Barò Santa Maria del Sepulcre 5 ☎ 971 710759 🕐 Closed Tue

Celler Sa Premsa (££)
Mallorcan classics in a converted garage lined with wine vats and faded bullfighting posters.
✉ Plaça Bisbe Berenguer de Palou 8 ☎ 971 723529 🕐 Lunch, dinner. Closed Sun

Chopin (£££)
Top-notch Swiss-Mediterranean dishes on a garden terrace in the back streets close to the Born.
✉ Carrer Ca'n Puigdorfila 2 ☎ 971 723556 🕐 Lunch, dinner. Closed Sun

Es Baluard (£££)
Modern versions of traditional Mallorcan cooking – how about shoulder of lamb stuffed with *sobrasada* and aubergines?

✉ **Plaça Porta Santa Catalina 9**
☎ 971 719609 🕐 Lunch, dinner. Closed Sun

Fábrica 23 (££)
One of the hottest restaurants in town is run by an English chef in the buzzing Santa Catalina district. Go early if you want a table at lunchtime.
✉ **Carrer Fábrica 23**
☎ 971 453125 🕐 Lunch, dinner, Tue–Sat

Fundació la Caixa (££)
Cocktails, cakes, sandwiches and serious meals in the bar of the former Gran Hotel.
✉ **Plaça Weyler 3**
☎ 971 728077 🕐 Lunch, dinner. Closed Sun dinner

Gadus (££)
Salt cod with everything is the motto at this offbeat fish restaurant in Santa Catalina.
✉ **Carrer Fábrica 5**
☎ 971 450162 🕐 Lunch, dinner. Closed Sun

Giovanni's (££)
This busy Italian restaurant near La Llotja has become a Palma institution, popular both with tourists and foreign residents.
✉ **Carrer Sant Joan 3**
☎ 971 722879 🕐 Lunch, dinner. Closed Mon

Koldo Royo (£££)
High-class Basque and Mallorcan nouvelle cuisine on the waterfront, with windows overlooking the bay.
✉ **Passeig Marítim 3**
☎ 971 732435 🕐 Lunch Mon–Fri, dinner Mon–Sat

La Lubina (££)
A fish restaurant on the quay – try *lubina en sal*, sea bass baked in rock salt.
✉ **Es Moll Vell** ☎ 971 723350
🕐 Lunch, dinner daily

Na Bauçana (£)
Friendly vegetarian restaurant with set-price midweek lunch.
✉ **Carrer Santa Bàrbara 4**
☎ 971 721886 🕐 Lunch Mon–Sat

El Pilon (££)
Good *tapas* bar in an alley off the Born.
✉ **Carrer Ca'n Cifre 3**
☎ 971 717590 🕐 Lunch, dinner. Closed Sun

S'Arrosseria (££)
Rice served in a dozen different styles, from 'convent rice' (vegetarian) to lobster *paella*.
✉ **Passeig Marítim 13** ☎ 971 737447 🕐 Lunch Tue–Sun, dinner Tue–Sat

S'Olivera (££)
Mediterranean cooking and a large range of *tapas* in the heart of the old Arab quarter.
✉ **Carrer Morey 5** ☎ 971 712935 🕐 Lunch Mon–Sat, dinner Mon–Fri

Sa Volta (£)
Authentic cellar bar with hams hanging from the ceiling – one of numerous *tapas* bars along the same street.
✉ **Carrer dels Apuntadors 5**
🕐 Lunch, dinner daily

Taberna de la Bóveda (££)
Great *tapas* on a terrace facing the harbour. The original La Bóveda is just around the corner at Carrer Boteria 3.
✉ **Passeig Sagrera 3** ☎ 971 720026 🕐 Lunch, dinner daily. Closed Sun

Tapas
Tapas are a Spanish institution. Originally a free 'lid' (*tapa*) of ham across a drink, nowadays they consist of small portions of everything from octopus to olives. Locals eat *tapas* before going out to eat, but several portions can make an unusual meal in itself. The best place to eat *tapas* in Mallorca is in the area around La Llotja in Palma.

Around the Island

Eating Out in Mallorca

The Spanish like to eat late – many restaurants do not even open until 1:30 at lunchtime and 8:30 in the evening, and fill up an hour or two later. It is a good idea to book a table in advance, especially in summer and at weekends. Formal dress is rarely necessary – even at the best establishments smart casual is the rule. And children are always welcome!

Algaida

Cal Dimoni (££)
Meat and blood sausages grilled over an open fire at the 'house of the devil'.
✉ Carretera Palma–Manacor, km21 ☎ 971 665035
🕐 Noon–midnight. Closed Wed

Ca'n Mateu (££)
Roast suckling pig and other specialities beside a pool and children's play area.
✉ Carretera Palma–Manacor, km21 ☎ 971 665036
🕐 Lunch, dinner. Closed Tue

Es 4 Vents (££)
Mallorcan and Spanish classics, very popular for Sunday lunch.
✉ Carretera Palma–Manacor, km21 ☎ 971 665173
🕐 Lunch, dinner. Closed Thu

Hostal d'Algaida (££)
Mallorcan cuisine in an old coaching inn – try croquettes of spinach with monkfish.
✉ Carretera Palma–Manacor, km21 ☎ 971 665109
🕐 Lunch, dinner daily

Artà

Café Parisien (££)
Coffee, pastries, salads and Mediterranean cuisine in an arty café on the main street.
✉ Carrer Ciutat 18
☎ 971 835440 🕐 Lunch, dinner. Closed Sun

Binissalem

El Suizo (££)
Swiss fondues plus French and Mallorcan cuisine.
✉ Carrer Pou Bo 20
☎ 971 870076 🕐 Lunch, dinner. Closed Tue

Cala Millor

El Pescador (££)
Harbourside restaurant specialising in *paella* and grilled meat and fish dishes.
✉ Port Cala Bona
☎ 971 586602 🕐 Lunch, dinner. Closed Wed

Cala d'Or

Blanco y Negro (££)
Stuffed squid and other seafood specialities served overlooking the marina.
✉ Marina de Cala d'Or
☎ 971 643465 🕐 Lunch, dinner daily

Port Petit (£££)
Seafood and unusual desserts in a smart restaurant overlooking the marina.
✉ Carrer Port Petit
☎ 971 643039 🕐 Dinner daily, Apr–Oct

Cala Rajada

Ses Rotges (£££)
Quality French cooking with prices to match at one of Mallorca's top hotels.
✉ Carrer Rafael Blanes 21
☎ 971 563108 🕐 Lunch, dinner daily. Closed Nov–Mar

Cala de Sant Vicenç

Cavall Bernat (£££)
Top-notch Mallorcan meat and fish dishes, such as spiced turbot and roast suckling lamb, together with a gourmet tasting menu.
✉ Carrer Maressers 2
☎ 971 530250 🕐 Dinner daily

Calvià

Ca Na Cuco (££)
Fresh, good-value Mallorcan cuisine. Popular with locals.
✉ Avinguda de Palma 14
☎ 971 670083 🕐 Lunch, dinner. Closed Mon. Dinner only Tue, Wed

Meson Ca'n Torrat (££)
Mallorcan classics like *llom amb col* and roast shoulder

of lamb in a rustic bar opposite the church.

✉ **Carrer Església 5** ☎ **971 670682** 🕐 **Dinner. Closed Tue**

Capdepera
Café de l'Orient (£)
Lively *tapas* bar on the market square. Each dish is available in three portion sizes.

✉ **Plaça de l'Orient 4** ☎ **971 563098** 🕐 **Daily 8AM–midnight**

Castell d'Alaró
Es Verger (££)
Roast lamb is cooked in a wood-fired oven at this farmhouse restaurant halfway up to the castle.

✉ **On the way to Castell d'Alaró** ☎ **971 182126** 🕐 **Lunch, dinner. Daily**

Deià
El Olivo (£££)
Fine *nouvelle cuisine* in a romantic setting – one of the best restaurants on the island for a special occasion.

✉ **La Residencia hotel** ☎ **971 639392** 🕐 **Lunch, dinner daily**

Es Racó d'es Teix (£££)
Creative Mediterranean cooking in an old stone house with a delightful shady terrace.

✉ **Carrer Vinya Vella 6** ☎ **971 639501** 🕐 **Lunch, dinner**

Jaume (££)
A Deià institution, offering unchanging Mallorcan dishes like *tumbet* and *frit mallorquí* in defiance of the trend towards new Mediterranean cuisine.

✉ **Carrer Arxiduc Lluis Salvador 13** ☎ **971 639029** 🕐 **Lunch, dinner. Closed Mon**

Mirador de Na Foradada (££)
Dine with a view of the northwest coast. Typical Mallorcan/Spanish cuisine.

✉ **Son Marroig, Carretera Valldemossa–Deià** ☎ **971 639026** 🕐 **Lunch, dinner. Closed Thu**

Sebastian (£££)
Modern Mediterranean cooking with an emphasis on fresh fish in an old town house with bare stone walls.

✉ **Carrer Felipe Bauza** ☎ **971 639417** 🕐 **Dinner only. Closed Wed and Nov–Mar**

Fornalutx
Ca'n Antuna (££)
Mallorcan cuisine on a shady terrace with views of orange groves and distant peaks.

✉ **Carrer Arbona Colom 8** ☎ **971 633068** 🕐 **Lunch, dinner. Closed Mon**

Inca
Celler Ca'n Amer (££)
This busy *celler* beside the covered market was chosen to represent Balearic cooking at the Expo 92 fair in Seville.

✉ **Carrer Pau 39** ☎ **971 501261** 🕐 **Lunch, dinner. Closed Sun**

Celler Ca'n Ripoli (££)
Founded in 1782 with dark wooden beams, chandeliers and wine vats around the walls. Mallorcan cuisine.

✉ **Carrer Jaume Armengol 4** ☎ **971 500024** 🕐 **Lunch, dinner. Closed Sun**

Jardines d'Alfàbia
Ses Porxeres (££)
Catalan game dishes in a barn beside the Alfàbia gardens.

✉ **Carretera Palma–Sóller** ☎ **971 613762** 🕐 **Lunch, dinner. Closed Sun dinner, Mon**

Cellers
A *celler* is an old wine-cellar converted into a restaurant specialising in traditional Mallorcan cuisine. Real basement *cellers* have wine vats to prove it, but nowadays the term is used for any old-style restaurant. *Cellers* are good places to go in order to try Mallorcan classics like *llom amb col* (pork wrapped in cabbage) or *frit mallorquí* (fried offal). The best *cellers* are found in market towns like Inca and Sineu.

Menú del Día
Most restaurants offer a *menú del día* at lunchtime – a set-price three-course meal with water or wine included. You won't get much choice (typically soup or salad, meat or fish and fruit or ice cream) but the food will be freshly cooked, filling and sometimes surprisingly good. A three-course lunch in a small rural town will often cost less than a single portion of *tapas* in Palma.

Montuïri
Puig de Sant Miquel (££)
Roast kid and other Mallorcan classics served on a terrace beside a hilltop hermitage.
✉ Carretera de Manacor, km31 ☎ 971 646314 ⏱ Lunch, dinner

Orient
L'Hermitage (£££)
Choose between a flower-filled terrace or a dining room full of antiques at this 17th-century manor house and hotel. The menu is based on fresh local ingredients.
✉ Carretera Alaró–Bunyola ☎ 971 180303 ⏱ Lunch, dinner daily

Hostal de Muntanya (££)
Pa amb oli at lunchtime and modern Mallorcan cooking in the evening on the terrace of this newly renovated hotel.
✉ Carretera de Bunyola ☎ 971 615373 ⏱ Lunch, dinner

Mandala (££)
Innovative French–Indian cuisine by a couple from Geneva, in a house at the very top of the village.
✉ Carrer Nou 1 ☎ 971 615285 ⏱ Jun–Aug, dinner Mon–Sat; Sep–May, lunch Tue–Sun, dinner Fri–Sat

Restaurant Orient (££)
Suckling pig is a speciality in this popular village bar.
✉ Carretera de Bunyola ☎ 971 615153 ⏱ Lunch, dinner. Closed Sun dinner, Tue

Palma Nova
Ciro's (££)
Pizzas and other Italian/Mediterranean specialities served on a terrace overlooking the beach.
✉ Passeig del Mar 3 ☎ 971 681052 ⏱ Lunch, dinner daily

Peguera
La Gran Tortuga (££)
Seafood and European cuisine is served on a terrace overlooking a pretty bay – you can order your meal then take a dip in the swimming pool while it is being cooked.
✉ Aldea Cala Fornells 1 ☎ 971 686023 ⏱ Lunch, dinner. Closed Mon

La Gritta (££)
Chic Italian restaurant with an emphasis on seafood.
✉ Aldea Cala Fornells 2 ☎ 971 686022 ⏱ Lunch, dinner daily

Petra
Es Celler (££)
Typical Mallorcan *celler* bar with an olive press and hearty peasant cooking.
✉ Carrer de l'Hospital 46 ☎ 971 561056 ⏱ Lunch, dinner. Closed Mon

Sa Plaça (££)
Prawns with chocolate sauce is just one of the old-style Mallorcan dishes being reinvented at this small hotel-restaurant on the main square.
✉ Plaça Ramón Llull 4 ☎ 971 561646 ⏱ Lunch, dinner. Closed Tue

Platja de Palma
Ca'n Torrat (££)
A treat for carnivores – hunks of meat are barbecued over a fire in the garden.
✉ S'Arenal exit from motorway ☎ 971 262055 ⏱ Lunch, dinner. Closed Wed

Rancho Picadero (££)
Specialises in meats cooked on wood fires.
✉ Carrer de Flamenc 1 ☎ 971 261002 ⏱ Lunch, dinner. Closed Mon

Pollença

Ca'n Pacienci (£££)

Sample the adventurous French-style cooking including duck in five different sauces.

✉ Carretera Port de Pollença
☎ 971 530787 🕔 Dinner only, Mon–Sat, Mar–Oct

Cantonet (££)

Italian restaurant featuring salads, fresh pasta and vegetarian dishes.

✉ Carrer Montesió 20
☎ 971 530429 🕔 Lunch, dinner in winter, dinner only in summer. Closed Tue

Clivia (££)

This popular restaurant is in an old manor house – the speciality is roasted sea bass.

✉ Avinguda Pollentia 9
☎ 971 533635 🕔 Lunch, dinner. Closed Tue, Wed lunch

La Fonda (££)

Large portions of rustic Mallorcan dishes like snails and roast kid in a house with wood-beamed ceilings and bare stone walls.

✉ Carrer Antoni Maura 32
☎ 971 534751 🕔 Lunch, dinner. Closed Mon

La Font del Gall (££)

French style in an intimate back-street restaurant close to the 'cockerel fountain' from which it takes its name.

✉ Carrer Montesió 4 ☎ 971 530396 🕔 Dinner daily, Apr–Oct

Il Giardino (££)

Italian specialities – veal with mushrooms, salmon with lemon sauce – on the square facing the church.

✉ Plaça Major 11 ☎ 971 534302 🕔 Lunch, dinner

Porreres

Centro (£)

Cheap and cheerful – Spanish classics served in an old theatre and church hall. Try to get a table on the small patio garden in summer.

✉ Avinguda Bisbe Campins 13
☎ 971 168372 🕔 Lunch, dinner. Closed Sat

Port d'Alcúdia

Bogavante (£££)

The rice and fresh fish dishes are especially good at this seafood restaurant facing the harbour.

✉ Carrer Teodor Canet 2
☎ 971 547364 🕔 Lunch Tue–Sun, dinner daily

Khum Phanit's (£)

This is a real surprise – authentic Thai cooking and extremely good value.

✉ Avinguda de la Platja 7
☎ 971 548141 🕔 Lunch, dinner. Closed Mon lunch

Port d'Andratx

Miramar (£££)

Lobster and seafood beside the harbour – take out a mortgage before eating here

✉ Avinguda Mateo Bosch 22
☎ 971 671617 🕔 Lunch, dinner. Open daily

Rocamar (££)

This is the place to try Galician and Mallorcan seafood specialities in a perfect setting at the end of the promenade.

✉ Carrer d'Almirante Riera Alemany 29 ☎ 971 671261
🕔 Lunch, dinner daily

Port de Pollença

La Llonja del Pescado (££)

Lobster stew is a speciality at this harbourside restaurant.

✉ Dique Moll ☎ 971 866504
🕔 Lunch, dinner.

Fish and Seafood

Mallorca's fish stocks have long been in decline and most of the fish on sale on the island is imported from mainland Spain and beyond. By law, restaurant menus should state whether fish is fresh or frozen – prices for frozen fish are invariably cheaper. Fresh fish is always excellent; specialities include lobster casserole, sea bass in rock salt and *greixonera de peix*, a hearty fish stew cooked in an earthenware bowl.

Olives

Olives were introduced to Mallorca by the Romans and have been used ever since – the oil for cooking and soap, the branches for firewood, the wood for carving into bowls and spoons. Almost every meal begins with bread and olives, for which you may pay a small charge. Bread and olives are also at the heart of *pa amb oli*, the favourite Mallorcan snack – bread rubbed with tomato, drizzled with olive oil and topped with ham or cheese.

Stay (£££)

This is a popular fish restaurant on the jetty – try the *parrillada*, a fish and seafood mixed grill.

✉ **Moll Nou** ☎ **971 864013** 🕐 **Lunch, dinner. Open daily**

Siurell (££)

Grilled meat is the speciality at this waterfront restaurant, in a tourist area at the southern end of the beach.

✉ **Carrer Cirerer** ☎ **971 865427** 🕐 **Lunch, dinner daily in summer**

Port de Sóller
Celler d'es Port (££)

Enormous helpings of Mallorcan classics like roast shoulder of lamb with oregano.

✉ **Carrer Antoni Montis 17** ☎ **971 630654** 🕐 **Lunch daily, dinner at weekends. Closed Wed**

Faro (££)

Fresh fish in a magnificent setting, high above the fishing port overlooking the sea.

✉ **Cap Gros de Maleta** ☎ **971 633752** 🕐 **Lunch, dinner. Closed Tue**

Portals Nous
El Bistro de Tristan (££)

More modest version of Tristan (► this page), run by the same chef and open at lunchtimes.

✉ **Puerto Portals marina** ☎ **971 676141** 🕐 **Lunch, dinner. Closed Mon and Nov–Feb**

Meson Son Caliu (£)

Typically Mallorcan with a good-value *menú del día*.

✉ **Carretera Palma–Andratx, km12** ☎ **971 680086** 🕐 **Lunch, dinner. Closed Mon**

Tristan (£££)

Nouvelle cuisine with a price tag attached – widely considered the best restaurant on Mallorca.

✉ **Puerto Portals marina** ☎ **971 675547** 🕐 **Dinner only. Closed Mon, except in summer**

Wellies (££)

Waterside haunt of the jet set, where designer shorts are the norm. Steaks, fish, international food.

✉ **Puerto Portals Marina** ☎ **971 683898** 🕐 **Lunch, dinner daily**

Porto Colom
Celler Sa Sinia (££)

Seafood specialities in a perfect waterfront spot.

✉ **Carrer des Pescadors** ☎ **971 824323** 🕐 **Lunch, dinner. Closed Mon**

Colón (£££)

One of the top restaurants on the island, beside the sea, with a terrace overlooking the fishing port. Modern Mediterranean cuisine.

✉ **Carrer Cristobal Colón 7** ☎ **971 824783** 🕐 **Lunch, dinner. Closed Wed**

Puigpunyent
The Rose (££)

This long-established restaurant beside the church offers European and Spanish cooking.

✉ **Carrer Galilea 24** ☎ **971 614180** 🕐 **Dinner only, Wed–Sun**

Sa Tafona (£££)

Creative new Balearic cuisine served in an old olive press at Mallorca's top country house hotel. The hotel also has La Gazebo, a poolside barbecue which is open in summer.

☒ Finca Son Net ☎ 971 147000 ⊙ Lunch and dinner daily

Randa
Celler Bar Randa (£)
Good-value Mallorcan cuisine in the village bar beside the church.
☒ Carrer Església 24
☎ 971 660989 ⊙ Lunch, dinner. Closed Wed

Es Reco de Randa (££)
Mallorcan and Spanish cooking in an old hotel at the foot of Puig de Randa.
☒ Carrer Fuente 13 ☎ 971 660997 ⊙ Lunch, dinner daily

S'Arracó
La Tulipe (££)
Modern European cooking in a New Age arty atmosphere.
☒ Plaça de Toledo 2
☎ 971 671449 ⊙ Dinner Mon–Sat

Santa Eugènia
L'Escargot (££)
French classics and a menu that changes regularly according to what is in the market.
☒ Carrer Major 48
☎ 971 144535 ⊙ Dinner Tue–Sat, Sun lunch

Santa Maria del Camí
Moli d'es Torrent (£££)
German chef Peter Himbert offers a personal interpretation of German and Mallorcan cuisine at this restaurant in an old windmill.
☒ Carrera Bunyola 75
☎ 971 140503 ⊙ Lunch, dinner. Closed Thu

Sant Elm
El Pescador (££)
Fish restaurant on the jetty with its own fishing boat and fine views of Sa Dragonera.

☒ Avinguda Jaume 1 ☎ 971 239198 ⊙ Lunch, dinner

Sineu
Celler Sa Font (££)
Traditional celler with wine vats lining the walls – very busy on market day (Wed).
☒ Plaça d'Espanya 18
☎ 971 520313 ⊙ Lunch, dinner daily

Sóller
Bens d'Avall (£££)
Creative Mediterranean cuisine in a fabulous setting on a terrace overlooking Mallorca's northwest coast. For a treat, try the seven-course gourmet tasting menu.
☒ Carretera Deià–Sóller, Urbanización Costa de Deià
☎ 971 632381 ⊙ Lunch, dinner Tue–Sun, Apr–Nov

Ca N'Ai (£££)
Fine food and elegant service on the terrace of a country house hotel surrounded by orange groves.
☒ Camí Son Sales
☎ 971 632494 ⊙ Feb–Oct, lunch, dinner. Closed Mon

Sa Cova (££)
Mallorcan classics (stuffed aubergines and rabbit with garlic) in a great position on Sóller's main square.
☒ Plaça Constitució 7
☎ 971 633222 ⊙ Lunch, dinner. Closed Sun dinner and Mon

Valldemossa
Ca'n Costa (££)
Mallorcan and Spanish cuisine in a converted oil mill.
☒ Carretera Valldemossa–Deià, km2.5 ☎ 971 612263
⊙ Lunch, dinner

Coffee and Liqueurs
In Spain, un café after the meal means only one thing: café solo, served short, strong and black, with sugar. Ask for a carajillo and it will have brandy added, or a bottle of coñac left on the table for you to help yourself. If the waiter brings a liqueur with your coffee, this is a copa, a treat on the house. Enjoy!

Palma

Prices

Prices are for a double room, excluding breakfast and VAT:

£   = under €60
££ = €60–120
£££ = over €120

These prices will be much lower if you book as part of a package holiday. Most hotels in the main resorts are block-booked by tour operators and it is through them that you will get the cheapest deals.

What Does It Mean?

All accommodation in Spain is strictly classified and graded by the government. Hotels are graded from one to five stars; *hostals*, with fewer facilities but often just as comfortable, from one star to three. A *hotel residencia* or *hostal residencia* is one that does not serve evening meals.

Arabella Sheraton (£££)

One of the top hotels on the island, with all the expected luxuries. Near a golf course, 5km north of the city.

✉ **Carrer de la Vinagrella, Son Vida** ☎ **971 799999** 🕐 **All year**

Born (££)

Two-star *hotel residencia* in a converted mansion near the Born. The best value if you want character in the old city.

✉ **Carrer Sant Jaume 3** ☎ **971 712942** 🕐 **All year**

Ciutat Jardí (£££)

One of Mallorca's earliest tourist hotels has reopened after a major renovation. The Moorish-style building is behind the beach, with fabulous views of Palma, a 1-hour walk around the bay.

✉ **Carrer Illa de Malta 14, Ciutat Jardí** ☎ **971 260007** 🕐 **All year**

Meliá Victoria (£££)

A huge modern hotel which dominates the harbour area. Most rooms have views of the cathedral and bay.

✉ **Avinguda Joan Miró 21** ☎ **971 732542** 🕐 **All year**

Palacio Ca Sa Galesa (£££)

A beautifully restored 17th-century merchant's house between the cathedral and the Arab baths. Rooftop terrace and the only indoor pool in the old city.

✉ **Carrer de Miramar 8** ☎ **971 715400; www.palacio casagalesa.com** 🕐 **All year**

Palau Sa Font (£££)

A 16th-century palace converted into a boutique hotel, with pink walls, wooden floors and a small terrace pool.

✉ **Carrer dels Apuntadors 38** ☎ **971 712277; www.palausafont.com** 🕐 **All year**

Palladium (££)

Good-value alternative a short walk from the city centre. Popular with Spanish businessmen.

✉ **Passeig de Mallorca 40** ☎ **971 712841** 🕐 **All year**

Pons (£)

Simple one-star *hostal* in an old Palma house, with rooms arranged around a central courtyard. A good budget choice with lots of character, decorated with antiques and modern art.

✉ **Carrer Ví 8** ☎ **971 722658** 🕐 **All year**

Ritzi (£)

Budget *hostal* centrally located for Palma's *tapas* and nightlife quarter.

✉ **Carrer Apuntadors 6** ☎ **971 714610** 🕐 **All year**

San Lorenzo (££)

Six rooms only in a restored 17th-century manor house, with a rooftop swimming pool and attractive garden, close to the old city.

✉ **Carrer Sant Llorenç 14** ☎ **971 728200** 🕐 **All year**

Son Vida (£££)

Exclusive hotel in a 13th-century castle with its own golf course, 5km north of Palma.

✉ **Urbanización Son Vida** ☎ **971 790000** 🕐 **All year**

Valparaiso Palace (£££)

Spectacular views over the Bay of Palma from this five-star hotel in Bonanova.

✉ **Carrer Francisco Vidal** ☎ **971 400300** 🕐 **All year**

Around the Island

Algaider
Raims (££)
Rural apartments around the courtyard of a 17th-century house whose owners produce their own wine. Breakfast is taken in a delightful garden of palm trees.

✉ Carrer Ribera 21
☎ 971 665157; www.raims.es
🕐 All year

Artà
Ca'n Moragues (££)
Just eight rooms and a heated swimming pool and sauna in this stylish renovated town house.

✉ Carrer Pou Nou 12 ☎ 971 829509; www.canmoragues.com
🕐 All year

Banyalbufar
Baronía (£)
Two-star *hostal* in a former mansion with courtyard, watchtower, swimming pool and sea views.

✉ Carrer Baronía 16
☎ 971 618146 🕐 Apr–Oct

Mar i Vent (££)
Wonderful views from the terrace of this family-run hotel. Swimming pool and tennis court.

✉ Carrer Major 49
☎ 971 618000 🕐 Feb–Nov

Binissalem
Scott's (£££)
Discreet British-run hotel, all antique furniture and Persian rugs, in a 19th-century town house on the church square.

✉ Plaça Església 12 ☎ 971 870100; www.scottshotel.com
🕐 All year

Cala Figuera
Villa Serena (£)
Simple two-star hotel, perfectly situated at the mouth of a pretty bay.

✉ Carrer Virgen del Carmen 37
☎ 971 645303 🕐 All year

Cala d'Or
Cala d'Or (££)
Ibizan-style hotel set among the pine trees overlooking the beach.

✉ Avinguda Bélgica 49
☎ 971 657249 🕐 Feb–Nov

Cala Rajada
Ses Rotges (££)
An old-style villa with a beautiful flower-filled garden and a Michelin-starred restaurant.

✉ Carrer Rafael Blanes 21
☎ 971 563108 🕐 Apr–Oct

Cala Sant Vicenç
Cala Sant Vicenç (£££)
This family-run seaside hotel near Pollença moved into the luxury bracket after a major renovation in 1996. Facilities include a sauna, gym and a heated outdoor pool.

✉ Carrer Maressers 2
☎ 971 530250 🕐 Feb–Nov

Deià
La Residencia (£££)
A pair of 16th-century *fincas* with terraced orchards converted into a luxury hotel which is considered by many to be the best on the island. Four-poster beds and teddy bears in every suite.

✉ Finca Son Canals ☎ 971 639011 🕐 All year

S'Hotel d'Es Puig (££)
The 'hotel on the hill' featured in a short story by Robert Graves and also in Gordon West's *Jogging Round Majorca*.

✉ Carrer Es Puig 4
☎ 971 639409 🕐 All year

Reis de Mallorca
Reis de Mallorca (Kings of Mallorca) is an independent group of 26 Mallorcan hotels. It includes some of the best hotels on the island, like Palacio Ca Sa Galesa in Palma, Son Net in Puigpunyent and Ca's Puers in Sóller, but also cheaper options like the Costa d'Or in Lluc-Alcari and the Mar i Vent in Banyalbufar. What they all have in common is individuality, architectural beauty and generally excellent cuisine. Reis de Mallorca hotels can be booked on ☎ 971 770737; www.reisdemallorca.com.

Monasteries
Several of Mallorca's former monasteries rent out old monks' and pilgrims' cells to travellers. You may not get a shower but you will find peace, a sense of history and unforgettable hilltop views. The best known, at Lluc, is now virtually a hotel; for real solitude head instead for the Ermita de Bonany (▶ 55), Puig de Maria (▶ 74) or the Santuari de Montesió at Porreres (▶ 67).

Formentor
Hotel Formentor (£££)
This was Mallorca's first luxury hotel outside Palma when it opened in 1929. It is a grand hotel in a beautiful setting between the beach and the pine woods, with acres of terraced gardens.
✉ Platja de Formentor
☎ 971 899100 🕐 Apr–Oct and Christmas

Fornalutx
Ca'n Verdera (£££)
An old stone house has been tastefully converted into a modern boutique hotel, a great place to relax among the orange groves once the day trippers have left.
✉ Carrer de Toros 1 ☎ 971 638203; www.canverdera.com
🕐 Mar–Oct

Inca
Monnaber Nou (£££)
This 13th-century manor house, in oak and pine woods to the northeast of Inca, has a name which means 'flowery fields' in Arabic.
✉ Monnaber Nou, Campanet
☎ 971 877176 🕐 All year

Lluc
Monestir de Lluc (£)
Comfortable accommodation in a former monastery – a popular base for walking in the Serra de Tramuntana.
✉ Lluc monastery
☎ 971 871525 🕐 All year

Lluc-Alcari
Costa d'Or (£)
Simple but perfect, in a magical setting above the sea. You can walk to the shore through the hotel's own pine forest.
✉ Lluc-Alcari ☎ 971 639025
🕐 Apr–Oct

Llucmajor
Son Antem (£££)
Luxury golf resort and spa hotel owned by the Marriott group, who are also building a timeshare village on the same site.
✉ Carretera Palma–Llucmajor
☎ 971 129100;
www.marriotthotels.com
🕐 All year

Manacor
La Reserva Rotana (£££)
This 17th-century mansion with its own golf course is typical of the new breed of upmarket rural hotels that are opening up in Mallorca.
✉ Camí de S'Avall, km3
☎ 971 845685; www.la-reserva-rotana.com
🕐 Feb–Nov

Orient
L'Hermitage (££)
Former convent turned into a country-house hotel, with swimming pool, tennis courts, sauna and a first-class restaurant.
✉ Carretera Alaró–Bunyola
☎ 971 180303;
www.hermitage-hotel.com
🕐 Feb–Nov

Hostal Muntanya (££)
A former walkers' hostel, recently renovated as part of the trend towards upmarket rural tourism.
✉ Carretera de Bunyola
☎ 971 615373 🕐 All year

Petra
Sa Plaça (££)
If you want to get away from it all in an authentic Mallorcan village, stay in one of the three rooms in this town house on the main square.
✉ Plaça Ramón Llull 4
☎ 971 561646 🕐 Closed Nov

Pollença
Juma (££)
This early 20th-century hotel on the main square has recently reopened its doors to cater for the growing numbers of people wanting to stay in inland towns. Eight comfortable rooms, decorated in antique style.
✉ Plaça Major 9
☎ 971 535002 ⏰ All year

Port de Pollença
Illa d'Or (££)
An old-fashioned hotel at the end of the promenade.
✉ Passeig Colón 265
☎ 971 865100 ⏰ Feb–Nov

Port de Sóller
Es Port (£)
Three-star family-run *hostal* in a 15th-century mansion with a private chapel in the courtyard. The bar has the biggest olive press you'll ever see.
✉ Carrer Antoni Montis
☎ 971 631650 ⏰ All year

Puig de Randa
Es Reco de Randa (££)
Three-star hotel and well-known restaurant at the foot of the winding road to the summit.
✉ Carrer Fuente 13 ☎ 971 660997 ⏰ All year

Santuari de Cura (£)
Rooms in the old monastery, with spectacular views from the terrace at dusk.
✉ Summit of Puig de Randa
☎ 971 120260 ⏰ All year

Santa Maria del Camí
Read's (£££)
British-run hotel and sophisticated restaurant in a magnificent restored *finca* on the road to Alaró.

✉ Carretera Santa Maria–Alaró ☎ 971 140261; www.readshotel.com ⏰ All year

Ses Illetes
Bon Sol (£££)
Delightful family-run hotel, arranged like a wedding-cake on several levels and cascading down a hill to its own private beach.
✉ Passeig Illetes 30 ☎ 971 402111 ⏰ Closed Nov

Sineu
Leon de Sineu (££)
Small three-star hotel in a converted town house close to the main square.
✉ Carrer dels Bous 129
☎ 971 520211 ⏰ All year

Sóller
Ca N'Ai (£££)
Four-star *hotel rural* in a manor house surrounded by orange groves.
✉ Camí Son Sales 50 ☎ 971 632494 ⏰ Feb–Oct

El Guía (£)
Old-style hotel/restaurant by the station. Excellent value.
✉ Carrer Castanyer 2 ☎ 971 630227 ⏰ Apr–Oct

Valldemossa
Ca'n Mario (£)
Charming family-run *hostal* filled with antiques. There is a good restaurant on the first floor.
✉ Carrer Uetam 8
☎ 971 612122 ⏰ All year

Vistamar (£££)
Luxuriously restored *finca* with rock gardens looking down on the tiny Port de Valldemossa.
✉ Carretera Valldemossa–Andratx, km2.5 ☎ 971 612300; www.vistamarhotel.es
⏰ Feb–Nov

Fincas
Many of Mallorca's *fincas* (country estates) have recently been converted into upmarket tourist accommodation, combining character (antiques and log fires) with modern amenities like swimming pools. Some, like Es Figueral Nou at Montuïri, have become hotels; others, like Sa Torre, on an old wine estate near Santa Eugènia, have been turned into apartments for rent. You can get information on *fincas* from the Associació Agroturisme Balear, Avinguda de Gabriel Alomar i Villalonga 8a, Palma (☎ 971 721508; www.agroturismo-balear.com) or from the independent association (www.fincaturismo.com).

Markets

Weekly Markets

Almost every town in Mallorca has a weekly market; most start early and wind up by lunchtime. The larger markets all follow a similar pattern – fresh produce around the main square, specialist food stalls fanning out from there, then cheap clothes, household goods and craft stalls for the tourists. The biggest market is on Thursdays at Inca; the most traditional is the Wednesday agricultural and livestock market at Sineu.

Palma
Llotja del Peix (Fish Market)

Get here early as the night's catch goes on sale and mullet, prawns, sardines and sea bass are hawked by women with operatic voices.

✉ **Es Moll de Pescadors**
🕐 **Mon–Sat 6AM**

Mercat Artesanal

Lively craft market on the Plaça Major, with buskers and open-air cafés.

✉ **Plaça Major** 🕐 **Mon–Sat 10–2 in summer; Fri, Sat only in winter**

Mercat Olivar

Palma's main market, in a hall near Plaça d'Espanya. Fresh produce on the ground floor, meat and cheese upstairs, plus cheap *tapas* stalls and a public library.

✉ **Plaça Olivar** ☎ **971 720315** 🕐 **Mon–Sat 8–2**

Pere Garau

Local farmers bring their produce - including live animals - to this lively market in the east of the city.

✉ **Plaça Pere Garau**
🕐 **Mon-Sat 7–2**

Rambla

It may not match its Barcelona namesake, but Palma's Rambla is similarly lined with flower stalls.

✉ **Passieg de la Rambla**
🕐 **Mon–Fri 8–2, 5–8, Sat 8–2**

Rastro (Flea Market)

A Palma institution which takes over part of the main ring road each Saturday morning. Plenty of bargains but lots of junk too.

✉ **Avinguda de Gabriel Alomar i Villalonga** 🕐 **Sat 8–2**

Santa Catalina

Fresh fruit and vegetable market just west of the city centre.

✉ **Plaça Navegació**
🕐 **Mon-Sat 7-2**

Weekly Markets Outside Palma

Alaró – Fri

Alcúdia – Tue, Sun

Algaida – Fri

Andratx – Wed

Artà – Tue

Binissalem – Fri, Sun

Cala Rajada – Sat

Calvià – Mon

Campos – Thu, Sat

Capdepera – Wed

Colònia de Sant Jordi – Wed

Felanitx – Sun

Inca – Thu

Llucmajor – Wed, Sun

Manacor – Mon

Montuïri – Mon

Muro – Sun

Petra – Wed

Pollença – Sun

Porreres – Tue

Port de Pollença – Wed

Porto Cristo – Sun

Pòrtol – Thu

Santa Eugènia – Sat

Santa Maria del Camí – Sun

Santanyí – Wed, Sat

S'Arenal – Thu

Ses Salines – Thu

Sineu – Wed

Sóller – Sat

Valldemossa – Sun

Vilafranca de Bonany – Wed

Shopping in Palma

Shopping Districts

The main shopping areas in Palma are Avinguda Jaume III for upmarket boutiques (leather, antiques, designer clothes) and the pedestrian streets around Plaça Major for small specialist shops. There is also a modern shopping mall and hypermarket complex, Centro Comercial Porto Pi, 2km from the centre.

Books

La Casa del Mapa
Books and maps about Mallorca.
✉ **Carrer Sant Domingo 11**
☎ **971 225944**

Ereso
A good selection of books about Mallorca in English and German.
✉ **Carrer Paraires 1**
☎ **971 710283**

Fiol
Palma's leading second-hand bookshop.
✉ **Carrer Oms 45**
☎ **971 721428**

Fundació la Caixa
Art books and posters in the ground floor of this modern art gallery.
✉ **Plaça Weyler 3**
☎ **971 728071** 🕔 **Mon–Sat 10–9, Sun 10–2**

Ripoll
Antiquarian books and prints.
✉ **Carrer Sant Miquel 12**
☎ **971 721355**

Department Stores

El Corte Inglés
Branches of Spain's leading department store. The Club del Gourmet has Spanish wines, hams and cheeses.
✉ **Avinguda Jaume III 15; Avinguda Alexandre Rosselló 12**
☎ **971 770177** 🕔 **Mon–Sat 10–10**

Food & Wine

Bon Vins
Excellent selection of Mallorcan and Spanish wines and olive oils.
✉ **Carrer Sant Feliu 7**
☎ **971 214041**

Colmado Santo Domingo
Fight your way past hundreds of hanging *sobrasada* sausages to find cheeses, fig cake and olive oil.
✉ **Carrer Sant Domingo 1**
☎ **971 714887**

Forn d'es Teatre
Art nouveau shopfront and the place to buy *ensaimadas*.
✉ **Plaça Weyler 9**
☎ **971 715254**

Forn Fondo
Bakery which has turned out *ensaimadas* since 1911.
✉ **Carrer Unió 15** ☎ **971 711634**

Frasquet
Go in here just to smell the melted chocolate.
✉ **Carrer Brossa 19**
☎ **971 721354**

La Montaña
Sausages, hams, cheeses and one of Palma's best window displays.
✉ **Carrer Jaume II 27** ☎ **971 712595**

Son Vivot
Mallorcan and Menorcan produce, including *sobrasada*, cheese and wine.
✉ **Plaça Porta Pintada 1**
☎ **971 720748**

Shopping Tips

Most shops are open from around 10 to 1:30 and 5 to 8 Monday to Friday, and on Saturday mornings. The exceptions are souvenir shops in the large resorts, which stay open every day, and the Gigante chain of supermarkets, open throughout the day Monday to Saturday. Larger shops accept credit cards and traveller's cheques, but it is always advisable to have some cash.

Arts & Crafts

Siurells
Siurells are clay whistles, which have been made on Mallorca since Arab times. They come in all shapes and sizes – the most common design is a man on horseback – and are painted white with flashes of red and green. They are cheap, children love them, and the artist Joan Miró was much influenced by their brightness and simplicity.

Craft Fairs
A *Fira del Fang* (Ceramics Fair) is held each March in the town of Marratxí and all of Mallorca's leading potters are represented. Prices here are much better than in the tourist shops. *Baleart* is a Christmas craft fair held in Palma each December, with stalls selling everything from pottery and handmade shoes to Mallorcan wines and *sobrasada* sausages.

Palma
Alpargatería Llinas
The best place to buy espadrilles (rope-soled shoes).
✉ **Carrer Sant Miquel 43**
☎ **971 717696**

Artesanies Pol
A good selection of ceramics and glass, centrally situated near the top of the Born.
✉ **Carrer Unió 13**
☎ **971 724299**

La Casa del Olivo
Wonderful olive-carver's workshop in an alley off Carrer Jaume II. The best buy here is salad bowls – they're not cheap but you're paying for old-fashioned craftsmanship.
✉ **Carrer Pescatería Vella 4**
☎ **971 727025**

Centro Pelaires
Wander the back streets of Palma and you come across numerous contemporary art galleries. This is one of the best, with work by Mallorcan and international artists.
✉ **Carrer Veri 3**
☎ **971 720375**

Fang i Foc
A good range of ceramics from Mallorca and the Spanish mainland.
✉ **Carrer Libertat 29**
☎ **971 455860**

Fet a Mà
As the name implies, everything 'made by hand'. Pottery and glass, both traditional and modern.
✉ **Carrer Sant Miquel 52**
☎ **971 711095**

Herreros de Vicente Juan Ribas
The best place to buy *roba de llengues*, patterned cloth made on the island for over a century. There is another *roba de llengues* shop, Juncosa, in the same street.
✉ **Carrer Sant Nicolau 10**
☎ **971 721773**

Majórica
Palma branches of Mallorca's leading artificial-pearl-maker.
✉ **Avinguda Jaume III 11; Plaça Mercat 9** ☎ **971 725268; 971 722919**

Midge Dalton
Palma's antique shops are perfect for browsing, and this is one of the best.
✉ **Plaça Mercat 20**
☎ **971 713360**

Natura
Mallorcan branch of a Spanish chain specialising in environment-friendly gifts – candles, wood, clothes.
✉ **Passeig des Born 9**
☎ **971 718252**

Orquídea
Cultured pearls – slightly cheaper than its rival Majórica.
✉ **Plaça Rei Joan Carles I 1**
☎ **971 715797**

Persépolis
High-class antiques on Palma's upmarket shopping street.
✉ **Avinguda Jaume III 23**
☎ **971 724539**

S'Avarca
Traditional Menorcan handmade sandals.
✉ **Costa de Sant Domingo 14**
☎ **971 712058**

Vidrierías Gordiola
The best choice of Algaida glassware in Palma.
✉ **Carrer Victoria 2** ☎ **971 711541**

Around the Island

Algaida
Vidrierías Gordiola
Glass factory and museum
(▶ 43) in a mock castle near
Algaida.

✉ **Carretera Palma–Manacor,
km19** ☎ **971 665046**

Inca
Munper
Mallorcan leather is rarely a
bargain these days, but this
is the place to go for a wide
selection of shoes, handbags
and belts – the factory has
another shop at Montuïri.

✉ **Carretera Palma–Alcúdia,
km30** ☎ **971 881000**

Llucmajor
Casa Ordinas
A master cutler produces old-
fashioned knives and tools at
remarkably good prices here.

✉ **Carrer Vall 128**
☎ **971 660580**

Manacor
Majórica
Shop here after touring
Mallorca's largest pearl
factory (▶ 60).

✉ **Avinguda Majórica 48**
☎ **971 550200**

OlivArt
Emporium where everything
is made from olive wood.

✉ **Carretera Palma–Manacor,
km45** ☎ **971 552800**

Montuïri
Orquídea
Large factory shop featuring
artificial pearls.

✉ **Carretera Palma–Manacor,
km30** ☎ **971 644144**

Pòrtol
Ca's Canonge
Large selection of pottery,
especially heavy brown-
glazed cooking pots.

✉ **Carrer Trinitat 61**
☎ **971 602361**

Ca'n Vent
Pòrtol is the best place to
buy traditional Mallorcan
pottery – of two good *ollerías*
in the same street, this is the
first one you reach.

✉ **Carrer Trinitat 39**
☎ **971 602456**

Roca Llisa
One of the best places to
buy *siurells* (▶ 106).

✉ **Carrer Roca Llisa 26**
☎ **971 602497**

Santa Maria del Camí
Ca'n Bernat
Master craftsman's
workshop turning out
imaginative local pottery.

✉ **Carrer Bartomeu Pasqual**
☎ **971 621306**

Santanyí
Ceramiques de Santanyí
Innovative ceramic designs
based on ancient Mallorcan
traditions.

✉ **Carrer Guardia Civil 22**
☎ **971 163128**

Sóller
Eugenio
Gifts carved out of olive
wood – salad bowls,
salt-cellars, chess sets.

✉ **Carrer Jerónimo Estades
11A** ☎ **971 630984**

Fet a Sóller
The shop inside the station
sells local produce and
crafts, including olive oil, ice
cream and orange
marmalade. Profits go to a
local workshop for disabled
people.

✉ **Estació de Sóller** ☎ **971
633942**

Wine
Mallorcan wines have
been growing in reputation
in recent years and several
bodegas sell direct to the
public. If you are lucky you
will be able to taste before
you buy. Among the best
producers are José
L Ferrer at Binissalem
(☎ 971 511050), Miquel
Oliver at Petra (☎ 971
561117) and Jaume
Mesquida at Porreres
(☎ 971 647106).

Parks, Zoos &
Activities

Family Outings

As well as the attractions listed here, children will enjoy visits to La Granja (►57) and to the various caves along the east coast with their phantasmagorical light displays (►21, 54). The Sóller train and tram ride (►71) makes a fun day out, and the beach at Platja de Palma (►64) is very child-friendly with its seafront 'train', shallow water and Red Cross beach stations. Another enjoyable activity for children is a ride around Palma on a *galera* (horse-drawn carriage). You can pick one up from the top of Costa de la Seu, beside the cathedral and Palau de L'Almudaina.

A Warning

The attractions listed on this page are among the most expensive in Mallorca.

Mallorca is well geared up for family holidays. There are lots of good sandy beaches with safe, shallow water and first-aid stations, and many of the resorts have crazy golf courses and pony rides. Some hotels have children's pools and many also offer nurseries and baby-sitting services, as well as children's entertainment. If this is important to you, check with your hotel or travel agent before you go.

Here is a selection of activities that will appeal to children.

Theme Parks

Magaluf
Western Park
'Crazy Wet West' is the slogan of this Wild West theme park, with cowboy and high-diving shows, thrilling water rides, playgrounds, fast food restaurants and video arcades.

✉ Carretera Cala Figuera ☎ 971 131627 🕓 May–Oct, daily 10–6

Waterparks

Magaluf
Aquapark
There are pools, slides, a 'water castle' and exciting rides at this long-established waterpark on the edge of town.

✉ Carretera Cala Figuera ☎ 971 130811 🕓 Jun–Sep, daily 10–6; May, Oct, daily 10–5

Port d'Alcùdia
Hidropark
A water-based theme park with activities for very

young children, as well as waterslides, wave pools and mini-golf.

✉ Avinguda Tucán ☎ 971 891672 🕓 May–Oct, daily 10–6

S'Arenal
(Platja de Palma)
Aquacity
One of the world's largest water funfairs, with enough thrills and spills to keep little ones happy all day. In addition to the water slides and wave pool there is a mini-zoo, a children's farm, parrot shows and an antique typewriter museum.

✉ End of Palma–S'Arenal motorway ☎ 971 440000 🕓 May–Sep, daily 10–5; Oct, Sun–Fri 10–5 🚌 23 from Palma via Platja de Palma

Zoos and Animals

Cala Millor
Safari-Zoo
Drive-round safari park with giraffes, zebra and monkeys plus a 'baby zoo' with young elephants and reptiles born at the zoo (►45). Arrive early to see the animals feeding.

✉ Carretera Porto Cristo–Son Servera, km5 ☎ 971 810909 🕓 Apr–Sep, daily 9–7; Oct–Mar, daily 9–5 🚌 Free bus service from Cala Millor in summer

Cales de Mallorca
Exotic Parque
Children love the performing parrots at this tropical garden close to the east coast. There are also flamingos and a children's zoo.

✉ Carretera Porto Cristo–Porto Colom ☎ 971 183492 🕓 Apr–Oct, daily 10–7; Nov–Mar, daily 10–5

Magaluf
Nemo Submarines

See the flora and fauna beneath the sea on a 2-hour exploration by mini-submarine from Magaluf. Very expensive.

✉ **Carrer Galéon 2** ☎ **971 130244** ⏰ **Mar–Oct, daily**

Portals Nous
Marineland

The entertainment here is provided by the performing dolphins, sea lions and parrots. There is also a penguin pool, a reptile house and a large collection of sharks and tropical fish, plus flamingoes, monkeys and an impressive aviary. Children can take a ride on a mock pirate boat and a miniature train. The little ones will love it, but their parents may not – especially if they are fond of dolphins. But whatever you think about animal shows, Marineland is a success – and the crowds it attracts mean that it is generating handsome profits, which are then put back into conservation programmes.

✉ **Carrera Palma–Andratx, km10** ☎ **971 675125** ⏰ **Apr–Sep, daily 9:30–6; Oct–Mar, daily 9:30–5. Closed mid-Nov to Christmas** 🚌 **From Palma, Palma Nova, Magaluf and Santa Ponça**

Porto Cristo
Acuàrium de Mallorca

Small aquarium with exotic fish from around the world including piranhas and electric eels. Next to the Coves del Drac (► 54).

✉ **Carrer Vèlla** ☎ **971 820971** ⏰ **Apr–Oct, daily 10:30–5; Nov–Mar, daily 11–3**

Santa Eugènia
Natura Parc

An easy walking trail leads around a wildlife park where Mallorcan farm animals can be seen, along with butterflies, black vultures and imported species like pelicans and Chinese geese. There is also a picnic area and café.

✉ **Carretera de Sineu, km15** ☎ **971 144078** ⏰ **Daily 10–7**

Mini Golf

Palma Nova
Golf Fantasia

There are mini-golf courses in many of the resorts, but this is one of the best, set amid waterfalls, caves and tropical gardens. There is a choice of three different circuits – or you can play all 54 holes. Even adults will enjoy it.

✉ **Carrer Tenis 3, Palma Nova** ☎ **971 135040** ⏰ **Daily, 10–midnight in summer**

S'Arenal (Platja de Palma)
Golf Fantasia

When you tire of 'fantasy golf' in Palma Nova, you can visit its sister course on the other side of the bay.

✉ **Carretera Arenal 56, S'Arenal** ☎ **971 743334** ⏰ **Summer, daily 9AM–midnight**

Museums

Sa Pobla
Ca'n Planes

The top floor of this colonial-style house has childhood toys and games, while the lower floor houses a contemporary art museum.

✉ **Carrer Antoni Maura 6** ☎ **971 542389** ⏰ **Tue–Sat 10–2, 4–8, Sun 10–2**

Looking After Children

Small children are particularly vulnerable to sun and need to be well protected: apply a high-factor sun block regularly, especially after swimming. If you need a child seat in your rented car, be sure to book it in advance and then check it carefully on arrival. The same goes for cots and high-chairs in hotels and apartments. Finally, don't forget to check that your balcony railings are secure.

Theatres & Concerts

What's On?
To find out what's on while you are staying, ask any tourist office for a copy of *Where To Go*, published quarterly in English and German. The *Majorca Daily Bulletin* also has daily listings. A monthly guide to events in Palma is published in Spanish and Catalan and available at tourist offices and hotels. Remember that everything starts late in Mallorca – opera at 9PM, theatre around 10PM and music any time up to midnight.

Palma

Auditòrium
Palma's main venue for theatre and concerts.
✉ **Passeig Marítim 18**
☎ **971 734735**

Castell de Bellver
Outdoor classical concerts on summer evenings.
✉ **Parc Bellver** ☎ **971 287565**

Centre de Cultura Sa Nostra
Programme of free events at this arts centre in an old mansion in central Palma.
✉ **Carrer Concepció 12**
☎ **971 725210**

Parc de la Mar
Free outdoor concerts (jazz, rock or classical) beneath the city walls in summer.
✉ **Parc de la Mar**

Teatre Municipal
Contemporary drama, dance, ballet and films.
✉ **Passeig Mallorca 9**
☎ **971 739148**

Teatre Principal
Nineteenth-century theatre with autumn and spring opera seasons.
✉ **Plaça Weyler 7** ☎ **971 725548**

Around the Island

Alcúdia
Auditori d'Alcúdia
A stunning new hall hosting concerts and drama.
✉ **Plaça de la Porta de Mallorca 3** ☎ **971 897185**

Cala Millor
Sa Màniga
New auditorium with regular concerts and exhibitions.
✉ **Carrer Son Galta 4**
☎ **971 587373**

Cala Rajada
Jardins Casa March
These gardens and sculpture park make a beautiful setting for a series of evening concerts each July.
✉ **Parc Casa March**
☎ **971 563033**

Deià
Son Marroig
Concerts on summer evenings in the gardens created by Archduke Ludwig Salvator. Venue for Deià's classical music festival.
✉ **Carretera Valldemossa–Deià** ☎ **971 639178**

Esporles
La Granja
Displays of folk music and dancing on Wednesday and Friday afternoons at this museum of Mallorcan traditions (► 57).
✉ **La Granja**
☎ **971 610032**

Pollença
Convent Sant Domingo
The cloisters of this 17th-century monastery make a delightful setting for Pollença's international music festival (summer).
✉ **Carrer Sant Domingo**
☎ **971 534012**

Valldemossa
Reial Cartoixa
Chopin festival held each August in the Carthusian monastery.
✉ **Valldemossa**
☎ **971 612351**

Costa Nord
Top names in flamenco, salsa and jazz perform here during the Mediterranean Nights Festival (summer).
✉ **Avinguda Palma 6**
☎ **971 616070**

Bars

Resort Bars

Bars in the main resorts change their names and identities so frequently that recommendations are useless – follow your nose and you will soon find one that you like. Many bars are foreign-owned, with German or British names, imported beer and satellite TV. A stretch of the Platja de Palma is known as *carrer de la cervesa* ('Beer Street') owing to the number of German bars; the British equivalent is in Magaluf.

Palma

The best places for late-night bar-hopping are in the streets around Plaça de la Llotja and the terrace bars along the waterfront on Passeig Marítim.

Abaco

Palma's most unusual bar – in a 17th-century palace close to La Llotja (▶ panel).
✉ Carrer Sant Joan 1
☎ 971 715974 🕓 7PM–2AM

Barcelona

Cool jazz bar in a basement beside Abaco.
✉ Carrer Apuntadors 5
☎ 971 713557 🕓 From 9PM; live jazz from 10PM nightly

La Bodeguita del Medio

Cuban food, rum and *salsa* music – an imitation of its Havana namesake. Go late.
✉ Carrer Vallseca 18
☎ 971 717832 🕓 From 10PM

Cappuccino Grand Café

The hippest meeting place in town in an old Renaissance palace with a shady courtyard and art gallery.
✉ Carrer Sant Miquel 53
☎ 971 719764 🕓 8AM–1AM

Cappuccino Grand Café

The original Cappuccino Grand Café, on the waterfront, is still a popular place to meet for coffee or late-night cocktails.
✉ Passeig Marítim 1
☎ 971 282162 🕓 8:30AM–3AM

Hogans

Palma's first Irish pub opened in 1996. Occasional Irish fiddling, popular with locals.
✉ Carrer Monsenyor Palmer 2
☎ 971 289664 🕓 Noon–3AM

Made in Brasil

Popular meeting-place for late-night cocktails, smooching and Latin dance.
✉ Passeig Marítim 27 ☎ 670 372390 🕓 Daily 8PM–4AM

El Pesquero

Former fishermen's bar, now a chic waterfront café with *tapas*, drinks and harbour views from a terrace.
✉ Moll de la Llotja 2
☎ 971 721079 🕓 7:30AM–late

Varadero

Trendy terrace bar at the end of the old quay, with great views of the cathedral when it is floodlit at night.
✉ Moll Vell ☎ 971 726428 🕓 9AM–late

Near Palma

Abacanto

Cousin of Abaco in a 19th-century mansion on an industrial estate in the suburb of S'Indioteria. It is difficult to find – take a taxi.
✉ Camí Son Nicolau, S'Indioteria ☎ 971 430624

Wellies

Trendiest of many bars by the ritzy Puerto Portals marina.
✉ Portals Nous ☎ 971 683898 🕓 Daily 9AM–midnight

Abaco

Push open a heavy wooden door in Palma's busy nightlife quarter and you enter a different world. Huge baskets of fruit cascade onto the floor; there are fresh flowers everywhere and a subtle hint of incense. You sip fruit cocktails by candlelight, while listening to classical music, then wander into the courtyard with its fountains and caged birds. The drinks are expensive, but everyone should go once.

Discos & Dinner Shows

Dinner Shows

A recent arrival in Mallorca is the 'themed' dinner show and spectacle, which can be anything from folklore and flamenco dancing to a medieval banquet complete with jousting and serving wenches. These shows are basically aimed at tour groups; you can book at any resort hotel. Don't go unless you are prepared to abandon your inhibitions and join in the fun.

Discos

Palma

Ib's

Palma's latest disco is directly beneath the seafront promenade.

✉ **Passeig Marítim** ☎ **971 733671** 🕐 **11PM–6AM, nightly in summer; Thu–Sat in winter**

Pacha

Young and trendy club where Palma's teenagers come to bop the night away.

✉ **Passeig Marítim 42** ☎ **971 455908** 🕐 **10PM to late; nightly in summer, Thu–Sat in winter**

Tito's

Not quite as young as nearby Pacha. There are six bars, a laser show and fantastic views over Palma bay. You enter via an outdoor lift from the seafront promenade.

✉ **Passeig Marítim** ☎ **971 730017** 🕐 **11PM–6AM; nightly in summer, Thu–Sat in winter**

Around the Island

Magaluf

BCM

Europe's largest and probably loudest disco, with laser shows, banks of video screens, a swimming pool and room for 4,000 people. The upper level is for the young-and-trendy crowd, while the over-30s gather downstairs. Big-name international stars give live shows here throughout the summer season.

✉ **Avinguda S'Olivera** ☎ **971 131546** 🕐 **10PM–5AM; nightly in summer, weekends in winter**

Platja de Palma

Joy

Loud, brash, late-night disco with regular summer visits from big-name DJs.

✉ **Carrer de la Missió de Sant Gabriel** ☎ **971 262007** 🕐 **11PM–6AM nightly in summer**

Port d'Alcúdia

Menta

Designed like a Roman temple around an open-air pool, it honours Alcúdia's history each May with a 'Roman orgy'.

✉ **Avinguda Argentina** ☎ **971 891972** 🕐 **11PM–6AM, nightly in summer, weekends in winter**

Dinner Shows

Around the Island

Bunyola

Son Amar

Spanish and Hungarian dancing plus lion-tamers, performing horses, flamenco and magic tricks in Mallorca's top cabaret show, in a 16th-century mansion, near Bunyola.

✉ **Carretera Palma–Sóller, km11** ☎ **971 617533** 🕐 **Apr–Oct, dinner from 8, show 9**

Magaluf

Casino Mallorca

A choice of gambling in the casino (passport and smart dress required) or the Paladium dinner show with dancing.

✉ **Urbanización Sol de Mallorca** ☎ **971 454508** 🕐 **Casino 8PM–5AM nightly; show Tue, Thu, Fri, Sat 10PM**

Pirate Adventure

Yo-ho-ho and a bundle of fun on a mock pirate ship – with lots of audience participation required. Don't say you weren't warned!

✉ **Carretera La Porrassa** ☎ **971 130411** 🕐 **Times vary**

Golf Courses

Palma
Son Vida
Mallorca's first golf course opened in 1964 on an exclusive estate above Palma. A second course, Son Muntaner, has now opened on the same site. Near by are two five-star golf hotels.
- ✉ **Urbanización Son Vida**
- ☎ **971 791210**

Around the Island

Bunyola
Son Termens
Attractive course on an old hunting estate.
- ✉ **Carrer de S'Esglaieta, km10**
- ☎ **971 617862**

Cala Millor
Son Servera
Nine-hole course amid pine woods by the sea.
- ✉ **Urbanización Costa dels Pins, 6km from Cala Millor**
- ☎ **971 840096**

Camp de Mar
Golf de Andratx
A challenging course with narrow fairways, lakes and sea views.
- ✉ **Carretera Camp de Mar**
- ☎ **971 236280**

Capdepera
Canyamel
A testing course with small greens, sloping fairways and sea breezes.
- ✉ **Urbanización Canyamel**
- ☎ **971 841313**

Capdepera
Large, fast greens and six lakes, beside the road to Artà.
- ✉ **Carretera Artà–Capdepera**
- ☎ **971 818500**

Pula Golf
Challenging course on a luxury golf resort between Capdepera and Cala Millor.
- ✉ **Carretera Son Servera–Capdepera, km3** ☎ **971 817034**

Llucmajor
Son Antem
Wide fairways, fast greens and hidden water hazards. A second course opened in 2001.
- ✉ **3km outside Llucmajor on the PM602 to Palma**
- ☎ **971 661124**

Magaluf
Poniente
Long and difficult course, with lots of lakes and bunkers.
- ✉ **Carretera Cala Figuera**
- ☎ **971 130148**

Pollença
Pollensa
A tight nine-hole course, with small greens and narrow fairways on a hill with views out to sea.
- ✉ **2km outside Pollença on Palma road** ☎ **971 533216**

Porto Colom
Vall d'Or
Set among pine trees close to the east coast.
- ✉ **Carretera Porto Colom–Cala d'Or** ☎ **971 837068**

Santa Ponça
Santa Ponça
The venue for the Balearic Open, featuring long, wide fairways in open countryside dotted with almond trees.
- ✉ **Urbanización Golf Santa Ponça** ☎ **971 690211**

Ses Illetes
Real Golf de Bendinat
Undulating course set among pine woods above the bay of Palma.
- ✉ **Urbanización Bendinat**
- ☎ **971 405200**

Golf in Mallorca
In 1976 there were two golf courses in Mallorca; now there are 15 and more are being built. All are open throughout the year, providing a refuge for golfers fleeing frost and winter greens elsewhere. The typical cost of a round is €50–60, though this is much reduced if you come on a golfing package holiday. Don't forget to bring a handicap certificate.

113

Watersports

Sailing in Mallorca
Mallorca has 41 marinas, 30 *clubs nautics* and mooring for 10,000 yachts. Yachts can be chartered locally and most marinas also have facilities for water-skiing and windsurfing. Highlights of the sailing year include the King's Cup in August, the Princess Sofía trophy at Easter, and the Rei en Jaume regatta in July when a flotilla of yachts re-creates the 185-km journey made by Jaume the Conqueror when he landed at Santa Ponça in 1229.

Sailing

Baleares Yacht Charter
Information on chartering a boat, with or without a crew.
☎ 971 727986

Escuela Nacional de Vela Calanova
The national sailing school in Cala Major runs courses, as well as giving advice on all aspects of sailing in and around Mallorca.
✉ Avinguda Joan Miró, Cala Major ☎ 971 402512

Sail and Surf Pollença
Prestigious sailing club and school on the northeast coast. Instruction is available both for beginners and for the more advanced sailor.
✉ Passeig Saralegui 134, Port de Pollença ☎ 971 865346

Cala d'Or Marina
☎ 971 657070

Port d'Andratx Marina
☎ 971 671721

Port de Pollença Marina
☎ 971 864635

Porto Colom Marina
☎ 971 824658

Porto Cristo Marina
☎ 971 821253

Puerto Portals Marina (Portals Nous)
☎ 971 171100

Reial Club Nautic de Palma
☎ 971 726848

Scuba Diving

Federació Balear de Actividades Subacuáticas
The clear waters around Mallorca are the perfect place for diving, especially in the small, shallow coves of the south and east coasts. The federation is available to give information and advice on all aspects of diving in Mallorca.
✉ Carrer Pere d'Alcàntara Penya 13, Palma ☎ 971 463315

Aqua Marine Diving
✉ Port d'Andratx
☎ 971 674376

Albatros
✉ Port Cala Bona, Cala Millor
☎ 971 586807

Octopus
✉ Port de Sóller
☎ 971 633133

Scuba Activa
✉ Sant Elm ☎ 971 239102

Unidad Costa Norte
✉ Port Adriano, El Toro, Calvià
☎ 971 232676

Water-skiing
Water-skiing equipment can be hired on the major beaches, including Cala Millor, Can Picafort, Formentor, Magaluf, Palma Nova, Peguera, Platja de Palma, Port d'Alcúdia and Santa Ponça.

Windsurfing
There are schools at several of the larger resorts and it is also possible to hire equipment without tuition. Beaches where windsurfing is available include Cala Millor, Cala d'Or, Can Picafort, Formentor, Magaluf, Palma Nova, Peguera, Platja de Palma, Port d'Alcúdia, Port de Pollença, Port de Sóller, Portals Nous and Santa Ponça.

Spectator Sports

Bullfighting

Bullfighting is considered an art form as much as a sport in Mallorca; the leading *matadors* are national celebrities and there are fights most days on TV. A bullfight begins with a horseback procession, or *corrida*, followed by the fight itself; the bull is softened up by *picadores* and then the *matador* moves in for the kill. Many foreigners detest the spectacle – but it is undoubtedly an important aspect of Spanish culture.

Palma
Plaça de Toros
Bullfights are held in this 1929 bullring between March and October. You can choose between a seat in the sun (*sol*) or the shade (*sombra*).
✉ **Avinguda Gaspar Bennazar Arquitecte** ☎ **971 755245**

Around the Island
Plaça de Toros, Alcúdia
☎ **971 547903**

Plaça de Toros, Felanitx
☎ **971 580557**

Plaça de Toros, Inca
☎ **971 540087**

Plaça de Toros, Muro
This bullring was built in 1910 inside its own quarry of white stone.
☎ **971 537329**

Cricket

Around the Island
Magaluf Cricket Club
Cricket has been kept determinedly going by a group of British ex-pats in Mallorca, who play local and visiting sides on their ground in Magaluf.
☎ **971 233262**

Football

Palma
Son Moix
The home of Real Mallorca FC, who play in the first division and reached the final of the European Cup Winners Cup in 1999. Matches are played on alternate Sunday afternoons between September and June. If you're a keen follower of European football, look out for games involving top Spanish sides like Barcelona and Real Madrid.
✉ **Camí dels Reis**
☎ **971 221221** 🚌 **No. 8**

Horse-racing

Palma
Hipódromo Son Pardo
Europe's first floodlit racecourse opened in 1965. Trotting races (*carreras*) are held around a 1-km track at 4:30 on Sundays in winter and 9 on Friday evenings in summer. Trotting is a form of racing in which the jockey sits in a small cart behind the horse and must prevent the horse from breaking into a gallop. It has been popular in Mallorca and Menorca for at least 200 years. If you go to a horse-race meeting, remember that betting is an essential part of the process.
✉ **Carretera Palma–Sóller, km3** ☎ **971 754031**

Around the Island
Hipódromo Manacor
✉ **Carretera Palma–Artà, km50**
☎ **971 550023**

Tiro Con Honda (Slingshot)
The Roman historian Livy wrote of Balearic slingshot throwers being employed as mercenaries during Hannibal's crossing of the Alps in 218 BC; a statue of a Balearic slinger in the S'Hort del Rei gardens in Palma is a tribute to their importance in Mallorcan history. The art of the slingshot has recently been revived; to see today's slingers, contact the Club de Honderos,
✉ Bar España, Carrer Oms 31, Palma ☎ 971 726250.

What's On When

Mallorcan Festivals

Find yourself swept along by the atmosphere of a traditional *festa* and you will get a completely different picture of Mallorca. Most are religious in origin and a few date back to the time of the Christian conquest. Every town and village has its saint's day, whose eve (*revetla*) is marked by a *verbena*, a street party with music, dancing, fireworks and fancy dress. Battles are acted out between devils and heroic women, or Christians and Moors; people prance about as horses, and a good time is had by all.

January

Cabalgata de los Reyes Magos (5 Jan): The Three Kings arrive by boat in Palma to distribute gifts to the city's children.
Sant Antoni Abat (16–17 Jan): Processions of pets and farm animals in Palma, Artà and Sa Pobla.
Sant Sebastià (19 Jan): Bonfires and barbecues in Palma's squares.

February

Sa Rúa (final weekend before Lent): Carnival held in Palma and elsewhere on the last weekend before Lent. It is marked by bonfires, fancy dress and processions of decorated floats. In Montuïri the Carnival is known as *Darres Dies* (Last Days).

March/April

Semana Santa (Holy Week): A week of solemn Easter preparation begins on Palm Sunday, when palm and olive branches are blessed at churches across the island before being taken home to adorn front doors. During Holy Week there are processions every day in Palma; the biggest procession is on Maundy Thursday. Other towns and villages have their own processions too. On the evening of Good Friday a figure of Christ is lowered from his cross in Pollença and carried down the Calvary steps in silence. A similar event takes place on the church steps in Felanitx.

May

Moros i Cristians (8–10 May): Mock battles between heroes and infidels in Sóller, commemorating a 1561 battle in which local women helped to defeat a band of Turkish pirates.

June

Sant Pere (28–29 Jun): Processions of fishing boats in Palma, Port d'Andratx and Port d'Alcúdia in honour of the patron saint of fishermen.

July

La Virgen del Carmen (16 Jul): Processions of boats in the island's ports, including Cala Rajada, Port de Pollença and Port de Sóller.
Santa Catalina Thomás (27–28 Jul): Homage to Mallorca's patron saint in her home town of Valldemossa.

August

Sant Bartomeu (24 Aug): Devil-dancing in Montuïri at one of Mallorca's oldest festivals.
Sant Agusti (28 Aug): *Cavallets* dances in Felanitx, with children dressed up as cardboard horses being chased by giants to the accompaniment of bagpipes, flutes and drums.

September/October

Harvest festivals including a melon festival in Vilafranca de Bonany (second Sun in Sep), a wine fair in Binissalem (last Sun in Sep) and a *botifarró* (blood sausage) festival in Sant Joan (third Sun in Oct).

December

Festa de l'Estendard (31 Dec): Palma commemorates the anniversary of the Christian conquest with a procession from the town hall to Mass at the cathedral.

Practical Matters

Above: *Windmill at Algaida;*
Right: *Sóller oranges*

TIME DIFFERENCES

GMT	Mallorca	Germany	USA (NY)	Netherlands	Rest of Spain
12 noon	→1PM	→1PM	←7AM	→1PM	→1PM

BEFORE YOU GO

WHAT YOU NEED

		UK	Germany	USA	Netherlands	Spain
● Required ○ Suggested ▲ Not required	Some countries require a passport to remain valid for a minimum period (usually at least six months) beyond the date of entry – contact their consulate or embassy or your travel agent for details.					
Passport/National Identity Card		●	●	●	●	▲
Visa (Regulations can change – check before planning your journey)		▲	▲	▲	▲	▲
Onward or Return Ticket		○	○	●	○	○
Health Inoculations		▲	▲	▲	▲	▲
Health Documentation (► 123, Health)		●	●	●	●	▲
Travel Insurance		○	○	○	○	○
Driving Licence (national with Spanish translation or International)		●	●	●	●	●
Car Insurance Certificate		●	●	●	●	○
Car Registration Document		●	●	●	●	○

WHEN TO GO

Palma

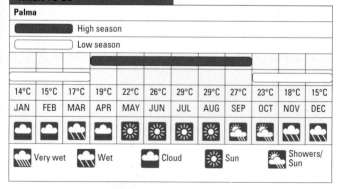

JAN	FEB	MAR	APR	MAY	JUN	JUL	AUG	SEP	OCT	NOV	DEC
14°C	15°C	17°C	19°C	22°C	26°C	29°C	29°C	27°C	23°C	18°C	15°C

High season / Low season

Very wet   Wet   Cloud   Sun   Showers/Sun

TOURIST OFFICES

In the UK
Spanish Tourist Office
22–23 Manchester Square
London
W1M 5AP
☎ 0207 486 8077
Fax: 0207 486 8034

In the USA
Tourist Office of Spain
666 Fifth Avenue 35th
New York
NY 10103
☎ 212/265 8822
Fax: 212/265 8864

POLICE (POLICÍA NACIONAL) 112

FIRE (BOMBEROS) 112

AMBULANCE (AMBULÀNCIA) 112

IN ANY EMERGENCY DIAL 112

WHEN YOU ARE THERE

ARRIVING

Spain's national airline, Iberia, has scheduled flights to Palma's Son Sant Joan Airport from major Spanish and European cities, but charter flights are much cheaper. Ferry services operate from the Spanish mainland, Menorca and Ibiza to Palma.

Son Sant Joan Airport Kilometres to city centre	Journey times	
	🚆	N/A
11 kilometres	🚌	30 minutes
	🚕	15 minutes

Palma Ferry Terminal Kilometres to city centre	Journey times	
	🚆	N/A
4 kilometres	🚌	30 minutes
	🚕	10 minutes

MONEY

The euro is the official currency of Spain. Euro banknotes and coins were introduced in January 2002. Banknotes are in denominations of 5, 10, 20, 50, 100, 200 and 500 euros; coins are in denominations of 1, 2, 5, 10, 20 and 50 cents, and 1 and 2 euros. Euro traveller's cheques are widely accepted, as are major credit cards. Credit and debit cards can also be used for withdrawing euro notes from cashpoint machines. Banks can be found in most towns in Mallorca. Spain's former currency, the peseta, went out of circulation in early 2002.

TIME

🕐 Like the rest of Spain, Mallorca is one hour ahead of Greenwich Mean Time (GMT+1), but from late March until late September, summer time (GMT+2) operates.

CUSTOMS

 YES

From another EU country for personal use (guidelines):
800 cigarettes, 200 cigars, 1kg tobacco
10 litres of spirits (over 22%)
20 litres of aperitifs
90 litres of wine, of which 60 litres can be sparkling wine
110 litres of beer
From a non-EU country for your personal use, the allowances are:
200 cigarettes OR 50 cigars OR 250g tobacco
1 litre of spirits (over 22%)
2 litres of intermediary products (eg sherry) and sparkling wine
2 litres of still wine
50g perfume
0.25 litres of eau de toilette
The value limit for goods is €175
Travellers under 17 years of age are not entitled to the tobacco and alcohol allowances

 NO

Drugs, firearms, ammunition, offensive weapons, obscene material, unlicensed animals.

CONSULATES

UK
☎ (971) 712445

Germany
☎ (971) 722371

USA
☎ (971) 722660

Netherlands
☎ (971) 716493

WHEN YOU ARE THERE

TOURIST OFFICES

Mallorca Tourist Board

● Fomento del Turismo de
  Mallorca
  Carrer de Constitució 1
  Palma 07001 ☎ 971 725396

**Local Tourist Offices
(Oficinas de Información
Turística – OIT)**

Palma
● Carrer de Sant Domingo 11
  Palma 07001
  ☎ 971 724090

● Parc de les Estacions
  Palma 07002
  ☎ 971 754329

Palma Nova
● Passeig de la Mar 13
  Calvià 07181
  ☎ 971 682365

Port d'Alcúdia
● Carretera Artà 68
  Alcúdia 07410
  ☎ 971 892615

Port de Pollença
● Carrer de les Monges 9
  Pollença 07470
  ☎ 971 865467

Sóller
● Plaça de Sa Constitució 1
  Sóller 07100
  ☎ 971 630200

Other offices include: Cala
d'Or, Cala Millor, Cala Rajada,
Cala Sant Vicenç, Ca'n
Picafort, Colònia de Sant
Jordi, Magaluf, Peguera,
Platja de Muro, Port de
Sóller, Porto Cristo, S'Arenal,
Ses Illetes and Santa Ponça.

NATIONAL HOLIDAYS

J	F	M	A	M	J	J	A	S	O	N	D
2		(2)	(2)	1			1		1	1	3

1 Jan	New Year's Day
6 Jan	Epiphany
Mar/Apr	Good Friday, Easter Monday
1 May	Labour Day
15 Aug	Assumption of the Virgin
12 Oct	National Day
1 Nov	All Saints' Day
6 Dec	Constitution Day
8 Dec	Feast of the Immaculate Conception
25 Dec	Christmas Day

Many shops and offices close for longer periods
around Christmas and Easter, as well as for the
festivals of Corpus Christi in May/June and Sant
Jaume on 25 July.

OPENING HOURS

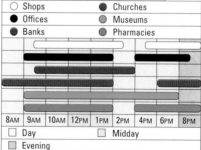

○ Shops	● Churches
● Offices	◐ Museums
● Banks	◐ Pharmacies

| 8AM | 9AM | 10AM | 12PM | 1PM | 2PM | 4PM | 6PM | 8PM |

□ Day □ Midday

▨ Evening

Large department stores, supermarkets and shops in
tourist resorts may open outside the times shown
above, especially in summer. In general, pharmacies,
banks and shops close on Saturday afternoon. Banks
close all day Saturday, June to September, but
stay open until 4:30PM Monday to Thursday, October
to May.

The opening times of museums is just a rough guide;
some are open longer hours in summer while hours
are reduced in winter. Some museums close at
weekends or another day in the week.

DRIVE ON THE RIGHT

TOILETS FREE

★★
★★

PUBLIC TRANSPORT

 Trains The main railway line connects Palma to Inca and Sa Pobla, with stops at Santa Maria del Camí, Binissalem and Muro. There are regular trains throughout the day, taking 35 minutes to Inca and 55 minutes to Sa Pobla (☎ 971 752245). Five trains a day leave for Palma for Sóller, beginning at 8AM (☎ 971 752051) and connecting with the tram to Port de Sóller (► 71). The two railway stations are found close together, beside Plaça d'Espanya.

 Buses A comprehensive network of buses connects Palma to Mallorca's main towns, with extra services linking the beach resorts in summer. Buses out of Palma depart from the new bus station on Carrer Eusebi Estada, behind Plaça d'Espanya. Palma has its own network of city buses, which also covers the beach resorts around Palma Bay (☎ 971 431024). Bus No. 25 is an express link between Plaça d'Espanya and the airport.

 Boat Trips In summer there are regular boat tours of Palma Bay and excursions from resorts including Cala d'Or, Port de Pollença and Port de Sóller. Some of these go to remote beaches which can only be reached by boat. There is also the day trip to Cabrera (► 46). One trip which runs throughout the year is the journey around the northwest coast from Port de Sóller to Sa Colobra (☎ 971 633109).

 Menorca Day trips to Menorca can be made on a fast catamaran, which leaves Cala Rajada at 9AM daily, arriving at the Menorcan city of Ciutadella in one hour. The return journey leaves Ciutadella at 7:30PM (Cape Balear ☎ 902 100444). There are also daily car ferries to Ciutadella from Port d'Alcúdia (☎ 902 119128).

CAR RENTAL

 The leading international car rental companies have offices at Palma airport and you can book a car in advance (essential in peak periods) either direct or through a travel agent. Local companies offer competitive rates and will usually deliver a car to the airport.

TAXIS

 Taxis can be hired at ranks (indicated by a blue square with a 'T'), on the street (by flagging down those with a green light) or at hotels. They are good value within Palma but expensive over long distances. A list of tariffs is displayed at taxi ranks.

DRIVING

 Speed limits on motorways (*autopistas*): **120kph**

 Speed limits on main roads: **100kph**
Speed limits on minor roads: **90kph**

 Speed limits on urban roads: **60kph**

 Seat belts must be worn in front seats at all times and in rear seats where fitted.

 Random breath-testing. Limit: 50 micrograms of alcohol in 100ml of breath.

 All hire cars take either unleaded petrol (*sin plomo*) or diesel (*gasoleo*). The top grade is *Super Plus* (98-octane), though *Super* (96-octane) is usually acceptable. Petrol stations are normally open 6AM–10PM, and closed Sundays, though larger ones (often self service) are open 24 hours. Most take credit cards. There are few petrol stations in the mountain areas.

 If you break down driving your own car and are a member of an AIT-affiliated motoring club, you can call the Real Automóvil Club de España (☎ 971 593 3333). If the car is hired follow the instructions given in the documentation; most of the international rental firms

121

PERSONAL SAFETY

The national police force, the Policía Nacional (brown uniforms), keep law and order in urban areas. Some resorts have their own tourist-friendly Policía Turística. If you need a police station ask for *la comisaría*. To help prevent crime:

- Do not carry more cash than you need.
- Do not leave valuables on the beach or poolside.
- Beware of pickpockets in markets, tourist sights or crowded places.
- Avoid walking alone in dark alleys at night.

Police assistance:
☎ **112**
from any call box

TELEPHONES

Most public telephones accept coins, credit cards and telephone cards (*tarjetas telefónicas*), available from post offices, news kiosks and tabacconists. Telephone numbers in Mallorca begin with 971; you must dial all nine digits wherever you are calling from. To call Mallorca from the UK dial 00 34; from the USA dial 011 34. To call the operator dial 002.

International Dialling Codes
From Mallorca (Spain) to:

UK:	**00 44**
Germany:	**00 49**
USA:	**00 1**
Netherlands:	**00 31**

POST

Post Offices
Post offices are generally open Monday to Friday, 9AM–2PM, but some also open in the afternoon and on Saturday morning. The main post office in Palma at Carrer de Constitució 5 is open Monday to Friday 8:30AM to 8:30PM and Saturday 9AM–2PM ☎ 902 197197

ELECTRICITY

The power supply in Mallorca is: 220–225 volts.

Sockets accept two-round-pin-style plugs, so an adaptor is needed for most non-Continental appliances and a transformer for appliances operating on 100–120 volts.

TIPS/GRATUITIES

Yes ✓ No ✗		
Restaurants (if service not included)	✓	10%
Cafés/bars (if service not included)	✓	change
Tour guides	✓	€1
Hairdressers	✓	change
Taxis	✓	10%
Chambermaids	✓	€1
Porters	✓	€1
Theatre/cinema usherettes	✓	change
Cloakroom attendants	✓	change
Toilets	✗	

PHOTOGRAPHY
What to photograph: mountains, hilltop monasteries, pretty mountain villages and attractive harbours.
Best time to photograph: the Mallorcan summer sun can be powerful at the height of the day making photos taken at this time appear 'flat'; it is best to photograph in the early morning or late evening.
Where to buy film: film and camera batteries are readily available from tourist shops and *drouguerias*.

HEALTH

Insurance
Nationals of EU and certain other countries can get medical treatment in Spain with the relevant documentation (Form E111 for Britons), although private medical insurance is still advised and is essential for all other visitors.

Dental Services
Dental treatment is not usually available free of charge as all dentists practise privately. A list of *dentistas* can be found in the yellow pages of the telephone directory. Dental treatment should be covered by private medical insurance.

Sun Advice
The sunniest (and hottest) months are July and August, with an average of 11 hours sun a day and daytime temperatures of 29°C. During these months particularly you should avoid the midday sun and use a strong sunblock.

Drugs
Prescription and non-prescription drugs and medicines are available from pharmacies (*farmàcies*), distinguished by a large green cross. They are able to dispense many drugs which would be available only on prescription in other countries.

Safe Water
Tap water is generally safe though it can be heavily chlorinated. Mineral water is cheap to buy and is sold as *con gas* (carbonated) and *sin gas* (still). Drink plenty of water during hot weather.

CONCESSIONS

Students Holders of an International Student Identity Card may be able to obtain some concessions on travel, entrance fees etc, but Mallorca is not really geared up for students, it is more suited to families and senior citizens. However, there are two youth hostels on the island, one near Palma and the other outside Alcúdia. Another cheap form of accommodation is to stay in a monastery; just turn up or book ahead.

Senior Citizens Mallorca is an excellent destination for older travellers, especially in winter when the resorts are quieter, prices more reasonable and hotels offer very economical long-stay rates. The best deals are available through tour operators who specialise in holidays for senior citizens.

CLOTHING SIZES

Mallorca (Spain)	UK	Rest of Europe		
46	36	46	36	Suits
48	38	48	38	
50	40	50	40	
52	42	52	42	
54	44	54	44	
56	46	56	46	
41	7	41	8	Shoes
42	7.5	42	8.5	
43	8.5	43	9.5	
44	9.5	44	10.5	
45	10.5	45	11.5	
46	11	46	12	
37	14.5	37	14.5	Shirts
38	15	38	15	
39/40	15.5	39/40	15.5	
41	16	41	16	
42	16.5	42	16.5	
43	17	43	17	
34	8	34	6	Dresses
36	10	36	8	
38	12	38	10	
40	14	40	12	
42	16	42	14	
44	18	44	16	
38	4.5	38	6	Shoes
38	5	38	6.5	
39	5.5	39	7	
39	6	39	7.5	
40	6.5	40	8	
41	7	41	8.5	

WHEN DEPARTING

- Remember to contact the airport on the day prior to leaving to ensure the flight details are unchanged.
- If travelling by ferry you must check in no later than the time specified on the ticket.
- Spanish customs officials are usually polite and normally willing to negotiate.

LANGUAGE

The language that you hear on the streets is most likely to be Mallorquín, a version of Catalan, which itself shares features with both French and Spanish but sounds nothing like either and is emphatically a language, not a dialect. Catalan and Spanish both have official status on Mallorca, and though Spanish will certainly get you by (it is still the language used by Mallorcans to address strangers), it is useful to know some Catalan, if only to understand all those street signs which are being slowly replaced in Catalan.

hotel	*hotel*	chambermaid	*cambrera*
bed and breakfast	*llit i berenar*	bath	*bany*
single room	*habitació senzilla*	shower	*dutxa*
double room	*habitació doble*	toilet	*toaleta*
one person	*una persona*	balcony	*balcó*
one night	*una nit*	key	*clau*
reservation	*reservas*	lift	*ascensor*
room service	*servei d'habitació*	sea view	*vista al mar*

bank	*banc*	credit card	*carta de crèdit*
exchange office	*oficina de canvi*	exchange rate	*tant per cent*
post office	*correus*	commission	*comissió*
coin	*moneda*	charge	
banknote	*bitllet de banc*	cashier	*caixer*
cheque	*xec*	change	*canvi*
traveller's cheque	*xec de viatge*	foreign currency	*moneda estrangera*

café	*cafè*	starter	*primer plat*
pub/bar	*celler*	main course	*segón plat*
breakfast	*berenar*	dessert	*postres*
lunch	*dinar*	bill	*cuenta*
dinner	*sopar*	beer	*cervesa*
table	*mesa*	wine	*vi*
waiter	*cambrer*	water	*aigua*
waitress	*cambrera*	coffee	*café*

aeroplane	*avió*	single ticket	*senzill-a*
airport	*aeroport*	return ticket	*anar i tornar*
train	*tren*	non-smoking	*no fumar*
bus	*autobús*	car	*cotxe*
station	*estació*	petrol	*gasolina*
boat	*vaixell*	bus stop	*la parada*
port	*port*	how do I get to...?	*per anar a...?*
ticket	*bitllet*	where is...?	*on és...?*

yes	*si*	you're welcome	*de res*
no	*no*	how are you?	*com va?*
please	*per favor*	do you speak English?	*parla anglès?*
thank you	*gràcies*		
welcome	*de res*	I don't understand	*no ho entenc*
hello	*hola*		
goodbye	*adéu*	how much?	*quant es?*
good morning	*bon dia*	open	*obert*
good afternoon	*bona tarda*	closed	*tancat*
goodnight	*bona nit*	today	*avui*
excuse me	*perdoni*	tomorrow	*demà*

Acknowledgements

The Automobile Assocation wishes to thank the following photographers, libraries and associations for their assistance in the preparation of this book:
BRIDGEMAN ART LIBRARY 56 La Vent Parmi Les Roseaux, 1971, by Joan Miró (Marlborough Graphics, London); MARY EVANS PICTURE LIBRARY 11, 14b; NATURE PHOTOGRAPHERS 13 (Kevin Carlson); SPECTRUM COLOUR LIBRARY 7, 17, 20, 24/5, 26, 48, 58/9, 63; www.euro.ecb.int/ 119 (euro notes).

The remaining photographs are held in the Association's own library (AA PHOTO LIBRARY) and were taken by P BAKER, except: H RAINBOW 75, 76, 85; J A TIMS 122a; W VOYSEY 9a, 15a, 27b, 35, 67, 79, 80, 91b.

Contributors
Page Layout: Design 23 Indexer: Marie Lorimer

Dear Essential Traveller

Your comments, opinions and recommendations are very important to us. So please help us to improve our travel guides by taking a few minutes to complete this simple questionnaire.

You do not need a stamp (unless posted outside the UK). If you do not want to cut this page from your guide, then photocopy it or write your answers on a plain sheet of paper.

Send to: **The Editor, AA World Travel Guides, FREEPOST SCE 4598, Basingstoke RG21 4GY.**

Your recommendations...

We always encourage readers' recommendations for restaurants, nightlife or shopping – if your recommendation is used in the next edition of the guide, we will send you a *FREE* AA *Essential* **Guide** of your choice. Please state below the establishment name, location and your reasons for recommending it.

_____

_____

_____

_____

Please send me **AA *Essential*** _____
(*see list of titles inside the front cover*)

About this guide...

Which title did you buy?
   AA *Essential* _____
Where did you buy it? _____
When? m m / y y

Why did you choose an AA *Essential* Guide? _____

_____

_____

_____

_____

Did this guide meet your expectations?
   Exceeded ☐   Met all ☐   Met most ☐   Fell below ☐
   Please give your reasons _____

_____

_____

_____

continued on next page...

Were there any aspects of this guide that you particularly liked? _____

_____

_____

_____

Is there anything we could have done better? _____

_____

_____

_____

_____

About you...

Name (*Mr/Mrs/Ms*) _____

    Address _____

_____

_____ Postcode _____

    Daytime tel nos _____

Which age group are you in?

    Under 25 ☐   25–34 ☐   35–44 ☐   45–54 ☐   55–64 ☐   65+ ☐

How many trips do you make a year?

    Less than one ☐   One ☐   Two ☐   Three or more ☐

Are you an AA member? Yes ☐   No ☐

About your trip...

When did you book? m m / y y   When did you travel? m m / y y

How long did you stay? _____

Was it for business or leisure? _____

Did you buy any other travel guides for your trip?

    If yes, which ones? _____

_____

Thank you for taking the time to complete this questionnaire. Please send
it to us as soon as possible, and remember, you do not need a stamp
(*unless posted outside the UK*).

Happy Holidays!